To Charlc

Happy belated birthday!
keep up the great work!

Mr. H

Mr. Humphrey's Book of Math Poetry II
Copyright © 2021
Michael J. Humphrey

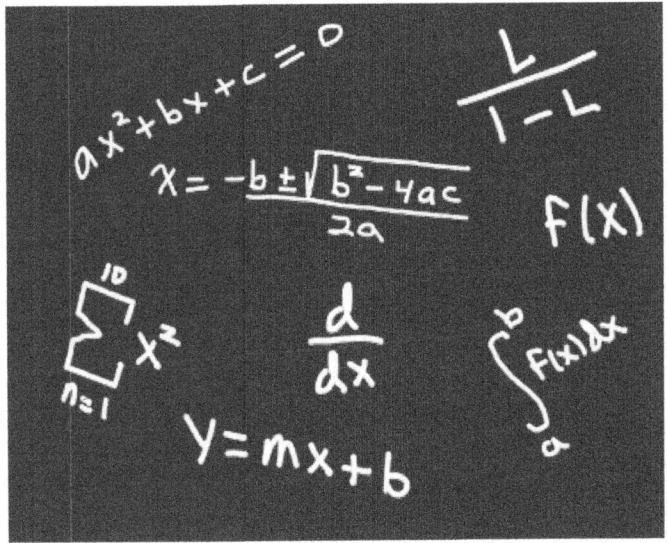

# Contents

Introduction ............................................ 6
Probability ............................................. 7
What are the chances? ........................... 9
Expected Value ..................................... 10
Counting Principles ............................... 11
Permutations .......................................... 12
Combinations ......................................... 13
Functions of Random Variables .......... 14
Quadratic Functions .............................. 15
Quadratic Formula ................................ 16
Complete the Square ............................ 17
Discriminant .......................................... 18
Transformations .................................... 19
Vertical and Horizontal Shift ............... 19
Reflections ............................................. 20
Vertical and Horizontal Dilations ........ 21
Circles .................................................... 22
Lines ...................................................... 23
Parallel or Perpendicular? ................... 24
Sequences & Series ............................. 25
Arithmetic Sequences and Series ...... 26
Geometric Sequences & Series .......... 27
Inverse Functions ................................. 28
Function Combinations ......................... 29
Functions Review ................................. 29
Compound Interest ............................... 31
X-Y Intercepts ....................................... 32
Factoring ................................................ 32
The Greatest Common Factor ............. 33

Factoring Trinomials ................................ 34
Exponential Functions ............................ 35
An Exponential's Inverse ....................... 36
Properties of Logs ................................. 37
Logarithmic Functions .......................... 37
Exponential Equations........................... 38
Quadratic Form Exponential .................. 39
Logarithmic Equations .......................... 39
Graphing Exponential Functions............ 40
Right Triangle Trig ................................. 41
The Six Trig Ratios ................................ 43
Angle of Rotation................................... 44
Standard Position Angles ...................... 45
Reference Angles................................... 46
Coterminal Angles ................................. 46
Trig of any Angle ................................... 47
Radians & Degrees ............................... 47
Unit Circle............................................... 49
Special Right Triangles.......................... 50
Point on the Terminal Side .................... 51
Graph of Sine and Cosine ..................... 52
Solving Trig Equations........................... 55
The Law of Sines................................... 56
Law of Cosines...................................... 57
The Sky is the Limit ............................... 59
The Derivative ....................................... 61
The Power Rule...................................... 62
The Product Rule ................................... 63
The Quotient Rule ................................. 63
The Chain Rule ...................................... 65
Higher Order Derivatives ....................... 66
Trig Differentiation ................................. 67

Derivative of e to the x ...................................... 68
Differentiating the Natural Log ......................... 68
Extreme Values ............................................... 69
Critical Numbers ............................................. 69
The First Derivative Test ................................. 70
Concavity ....................................................... 71
2nd Derivative Test ........................................ 73
Point of Inflection, POI ................................... 74
Students Welcome! .......................................... 75
The AntiDerivative .......................................... 77
The Definite Integral ....................................... 78
U- Substitution ............................................... 79
Integrating the Exponential Function ............... 80
Integrating the Natural Log .............................. 81
Trig Integration ............................................... 81
Appendix: Study Tips that Work! ...................... 83

# Introduction

My name is Michael Humphrey. I've been a high school math teacher for almost 30 years. I like to write math poetry, and use the poems as lesson icebreakers when I teach.

In the back of this book is an appendix with study tips. Many years of experience have gone into these tips, and throughout the years, many former students have come back to thank me for how well my tips had worked for them while attending college.

Below is an illustration of me as a math wizard created by Rooselan Vang, one of my former students. Thank you, Rooselan, for the illustration and for also including my secret greeting "Taerg si Htam!" ("math is great" spelled backwards)!

I hope you enjoy my book, and Taerg si Htam! to all!

# Probability

To measure chance mathematically
We need to learn to count
To compute a probability
We need to know the amount

The Sample Space we count it out
The events are counted too
The probability's without doubt
The ratio of the two

Independent? Not affected
By whatever happened before
Probability is unaffected
No need to keep the score

Union is "or" intersection is "and"
Some words to help us through
Count them out like grains of sand
Some formulas will help you too

Certain events are complimentary
They're either false or true
This may seem like elementary
Because they add up to one too

The sample space let's count it out
Events, we'll count them too
The probability is without a doubt
The ratio of the two!

# Probability:

A mathematical measurement for the chance that a certain event will happen.

# Notation:

$n(E)$ = the total number of ways a particular event can occur. Sometimes this is referred to as the event space.

$n(S)$ = the total number of possible things that can happen, some books call this the sample space.

$$P(E) = \frac{n(E)}{n(S)}$$

The probability of an event occurring equals the number of elements in the event space divided by the total number of elements in the sample space.

## What are the chances?

A 90 percent chance of snow in the morning
We want to know our chances
Of having a snow day with all its glory
And celebrating with dances

The chance is zero, I'll tell you why
It's something we call D-L
So be prepared and do not cry
I know you get the deal

So time to learn to measure chance
Probability is the key
For winning prizes and going to dances
Or living happily

Just take the number of desired events
And count them carefully
Divide by the total possible then
The probability you can see

So know the chances, figure it out
It's likely you will see
Just work hard from here throughout
To learn Probability!

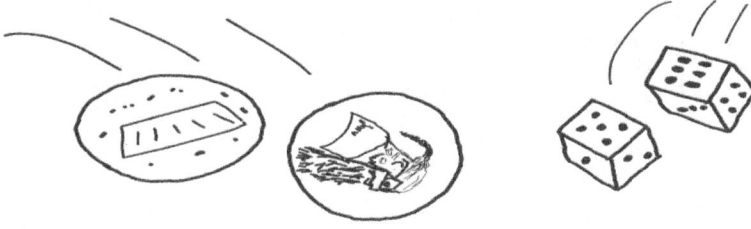

What are the chances?

# Expected Value

I took a dollar, went to the store
A scratch-off ticket I bought
Will I lose or win much more?
Dreams of it entered my thoughts

With so many prizes to win
A probability for each one
I'll sure be richer than I've ever been
Scratch-off tickets are fun!

So I multiplied each money prize
By the chance of that big win
Then summed it up to my surprise
The expected amount is in

An expected value or average win
Of 75 cents each try
But if I pay a dollar then
A quarter is lost by the side

A quarter here, a quarter there
Is this some kind of joke?
Because of Math, we're now aware
Those tickets will make you broke!

Expected value of a lottery
ticket that cost $1.00

| Prize | Prob |
|-------|------|
| 35,000 | $1/100,000$ |
| 1000 | $1/10,000$ |
| 100 | $1/1000$ |
| 10 | $1/100$ |
| 1 | $1/10$ |

$$Ev = (35,000)\left(\tfrac{1}{100,000}\right) + (1000)\left(\tfrac{1}{10,000}\right) + (100)\left(\tfrac{1}{1000}\right) + (10)\left(\tfrac{1}{100}\right) + (1)\left(\tfrac{1}{10}\right)$$

$$= .75\text{¢ average per ticket}$$

Because the ticket cost $1.00, the customer
will lose an average of .25 cents per ticket.

# Counting Principles

How many possible computer passwords?
We need a way to know
Or different types of tasty burgers?
Or various types of codes?

A fundamental concern in probability
Is learning how to count
The number of ways the event can be
And knowing the amount

If we know the ways events can occur
In sequence or together
Just multiply the ways together I heard
You've counted to the letter

Mutually Exclusive means separately
They can't happen at the same time
It helps to know this when counting you'll see
Just add them up, you'll do fine

Non-Mutually Exclusive, you have to take care
They can happen together at once
So don't double-count, you have to beware
When counting before lunch

Dependent events, connected you'll see
Probabilities, they will change
It's just a technicality
I know it may sound strange

Independent events are unconnected
To whatever happened before
Probabilities here are unaffected
No need to keep the score

So learn to count the number of ways
Each event can occur indeed
Then everyone will hear you say
I love Probability!

# Permutations

An ordered arrangement of a set
We call a permutation
Count them all, see what you get
Just do the computation

How many ways of choosing a winner
From everyone running a race?
Or different plates or types of dinner
From all the choices we can make?

ABC or CBA?
A three-letter permutation
How many ordered arrangements today?
To count while on vacation

Let "n" be the number objects to choose
When taken "r" at a time
A very convenient formula to use
For counting the objects in line

Take n-factorial, something to use
And don't forget to divide
By (n minus r) factorial too
The permutations cannot hide

How many ordered arrangements made?
How many permutations?
How many outcomes when running a race?
Let's do the calculation

Use the formula for ways to choose
The number of permutations
Just count them up, it' something to do
Then go on that vacation!

Example: How many arrangments of two letters can be taken from the four letters A, B, C, and D?

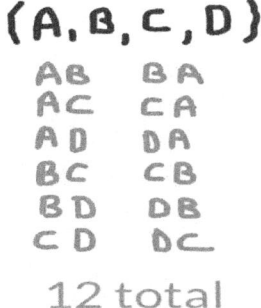

AB    BA
AC    CA
AD    DA
BC    CB
BD    DB
CD    DC

Using the Fundamental Counting Principle, the total number of ways of choosing the first letter times the number of ways of choosing the second.

$$4 \quad 3 = 12$$

12 total

## Combinations

Pepperoni-Sausage, Sausage Pepperoni
Two pizzas on the menu
Same kind of pizza says my uncle Tony
They're making it look like there's two

Different orders, toppings the same
We count them all as one
A combination is the name
A way to count that's fun

So then I counted all the platters
It took me several days
The order didn't really matter
Just items rearranged

So I took the menu, laid it down
Then, I called the waiter
Everything here's the same, I found
I think I'll see you later!

# Functions of Random Variables

A function of a random variable
To find probability
Out of how many is the scenario
For computing the chances you'll see

So I flipped a coin fifty times
Something I wanted to see
How many out of fifty I'll find?
What are the chances to be?

Just take the probability of success
Its exponent is how many
Times the probability of failure next
To the power of the number, if any

Multiply the result by n-C-r
The chance of r out of n
The random variable gets us far
Probability is found in the end

So 3 out of 5, or 5 out of 9
What's the probability?
A random variable helps us find
The chances for you and for me!

Hank Wilson has a batting average of 300. Assuming
that the probability of getting a hit is equal to his
batting average, find the probabilty that that he gets
3 hits out of the next 5 times at bat.

The exponent is how many

$$P(\tfrac{r}{n}) = {_n}C_r \, P^r(1-P)^{n-r}$$

$$n = 5$$
$$r = 3$$
$$P = .3 \quad \text{probability of a hit}$$
$$1-P = .7 \quad \text{probability of not getting a hit}$$

$$P(\tfrac{3}{5}) = {_5}C_3 (.3)^3 (.7)^2$$

probability of getting a hit

probability of not getting a hit

$$= .1323$$

did on calculator

# Quadratic Functions

A degree of two, a function too
A song that sounds dramatic
I'm telling you it's nothing new
We call this one quadratic

A special shape, a special name
We call this function's graph
The path of a ball is just the same
As a parabola on its path

A symmetry axis cuts on through
A point we call its vertex
A min or a max we call it too
With practice you can work this

A special formula finds the roots
It has a special song
With a, b, c you'll find them too
I know it won't take long

Standard form for sketching graphs
You'll find the vertex there
An important skill that you must have
You must complete the square

Oh quadratic, second in degree
Please listen to this verse
You model problems mathematically
And for that you come in first!

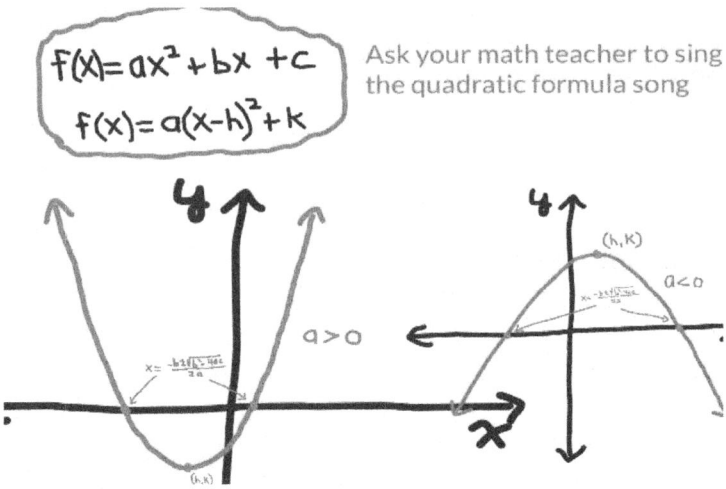

$$f(x) = ax^2 + bx + c$$
$$f(x) = a(x-h)^2 + k$$

Ask your math teacher to sing the quadratic formula song

## Quadratic Formula

A shortcut to completing the square
For finding roots of quads
The quadratic formula gets us there
For that we must applaud

"a" the coefficient of squared x
"b" from the linear term
The constant "c" completes the quest
For all who are concerned

It's negative "b" plus or minus
Square root of the discriminant
Divide by "2a" the roots you'll find us
This formula makes it imminent

It has a song, it has a ring
To help you memorize
Pop goes the weasel we will sing
The roots are the surprise!

16

# Complete the Square

A way to find quadratic roots
Oh yes without much care
We have a special way for you
It's called complete the square

Move the constant we call c
To the other side
Divide by "a" and carefully
Complete the square tonight

A perfect square trinomial
We factor without care
We write the squared binomial
Upon the paper there

Take the square root of both sides
Don't forget the plus or minus
One more step completes the ride
To put this all behind us

We found the roots but that's not all
Because we know about translations
Vertex form is now on call
We see all the transformations!

Solve the quadratic by
completing the square

$$x^2 - 12x + 9 = 0$$
$$x^2 - 12x = -9$$
$$x^2 - 12x + 36 = -9 + 36$$
$$(x-6)^2 = 27$$
$$x - 6 = \pm\sqrt{27}$$

$$x = 6 \pm \sqrt{27}$$

$$x = 6 \pm 3\sqrt{3}$$

17

# Discriminant

In life we have inequities and discrimination
Divisions, roots, and multiplication too
With pain we turn to demonstration
To change the things that we all do

Now thanks to math this world is better
Because math does not discriminate
Instead it uses the quad form letters
To find the quads discriminant

Real or imaginary? comes to mind
When finding roots of quads
The discriminant surely helps us find
The type of roots with awe

It's b squared minus 4ac
From the quadratic formula
It's all you need, just wait and see
You'll know the roots and form of them

Discrimination in life, yes it's wrong
But in math we have an answer
Use the discriminant to sing along
And then we'll have more dancers!

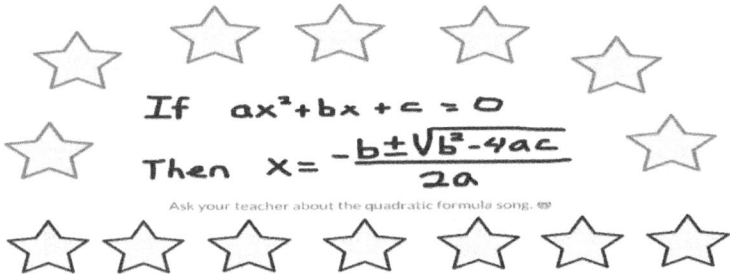

If $ax^2 + bx + c = 0$

Then $x = \dfrac{-b \pm \sqrt{b^2 - 4ac}}{2a}$

Ask your teacher about the quadratic formula song.

# Transformations

Translations move the graph around
According to some rules
Horizontally or vertically, they don't make a sound
We learn them all at school

Sometimes we compress, and then we stretch
Horizontally and vertically too
Then we reflect over y, then x
It's something that we do

The graph transformed in one, two, three
According to some rules
Please learn them all and then you'll see
The fact that they are cool!


# Vertical and Horizontal Shift

To the function, add or subtract
A constant, call it c
A vertical shift, upon the graph
It's something you must see

To the input, add or subtract
Another constant c
A horizontal shift is just a fact
In the direction oppositely

A graphing utility will help you fly
Through translations in this unit
You won't even need to wonder why
How tightly you fine-tuned it!

19

## Reflections

Multiply the function by negative one
To reflect it over x
Just give it a try and have some fun
And let me tell you next

If instead we multiply
A negative to the input
It now reflects across the y
Reflections never stay put!

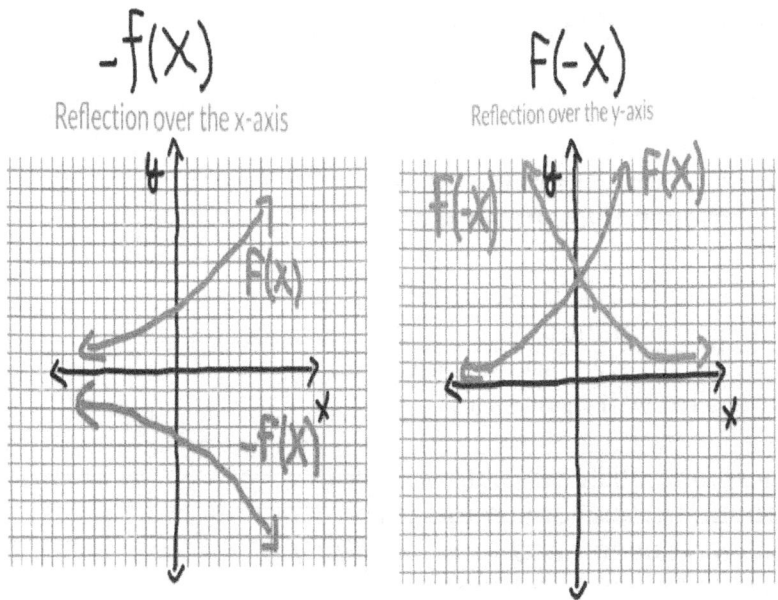

Algebraic Rules for Reflections of Functions

$-f(x)$
Reflection over the x-axis

$F(-x)$
Reflection over the y-axis

# Vertical and Horizontal Dilations

Sometimes we stretch, or maybe we shrink
A parent functions graph
The new-found shape we now must think
It's what we study last

Dilation's the name. It's what we call
This type of transformation
To stretch or shrink, it says it all
No matter the occasion

To stretch of shrink vertically
This is what you do
Multiply the function and then you'll see
It surely will come true

For horizontal this one's fun
But something different too
Multiply the input is how it's done
It's something you can do!

$F(x) + k$      Vertical Shift up by k.

$f(x) - k$      Vertical Shift down by k.

$f(x+h)$      Horizontal Shift to the left by h.

$f(x-h)$      Horizontal Shift to the right by h.

$af(x)$      Vertical Dilation with factor of a.

$f(ax)$      Horizontal Dilation with factor 1/a.

# Circles

Equidistant from the center
All such ordered pairs
Into my thoughts a circle entered
A standard form is there

The distance formula is what we use
When deriving standard form
With h-k center and x-y too
The standard form is born

From standard form we find the center
Then plot it on the graph
Four more points we now can enter
The radius gives us that

Restorative practice a circle too
Yes, things will come around
You treat all others like they were you
And peace will then abound!

Use the distance formula to find the standard form equation of a circle.

$$d = \sqrt{\left(x_2 - x_1\right)^2 + \left(y_2 - y_1\right)^2}$$

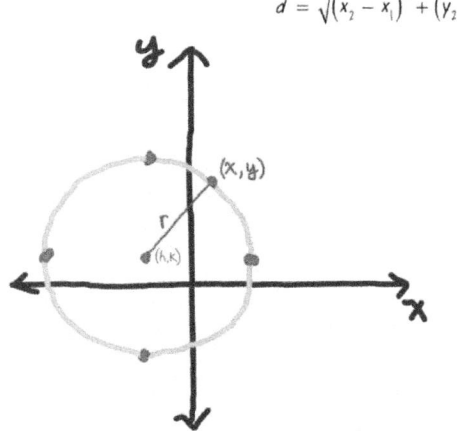

The set of all points a distance r, from the center (h, k).

$$r = \sqrt{(x-h)^2 + (y-k)^2}$$

The standard form equation for a circle with radius r, and center (h,k).

$$r^2 = (x-h)^2 + (y-k)^2$$

# Lines

Slope-Intercept and Standard Form
Equations of a Line
Point-Slope form is now the norm
A favorite one of mine

Between two points you'll find the slope
That some call rate of change
Rise over run is not a joke
Though it might sound strange

A point and slope you'll substitute
Inside the point-slope form
You'll solve for y, this constitutes
A slope-intercept that's born

Rise over run makes easy to graph
It's something we can do
Go up and over, and find points fast
A line will go right through

x equals k, a vertical line
A special case for you
Horizontal lines are just as fine
Because y equals k comes true

Equations of lines with multiple forms
No need to be concerned
A little practice to weather the storm
Is all it takes to learn!

# Parallel or Perpendicular?

We've compared the slopes of our two lines
It's nothing in particular
It's all we need so we can find
If parallel or perpendicular!

Negative reciprocal if we find
When comparing our two slopes
They're perpendicular, a pair of lines
Remember to take notes

Parallel lines an easy one
The slopes are just the same
Just write it down and have some fun
It's how we win the game!

Parallel lines have equal slopes

Perpendicular lines have opposite reciprocal slopes

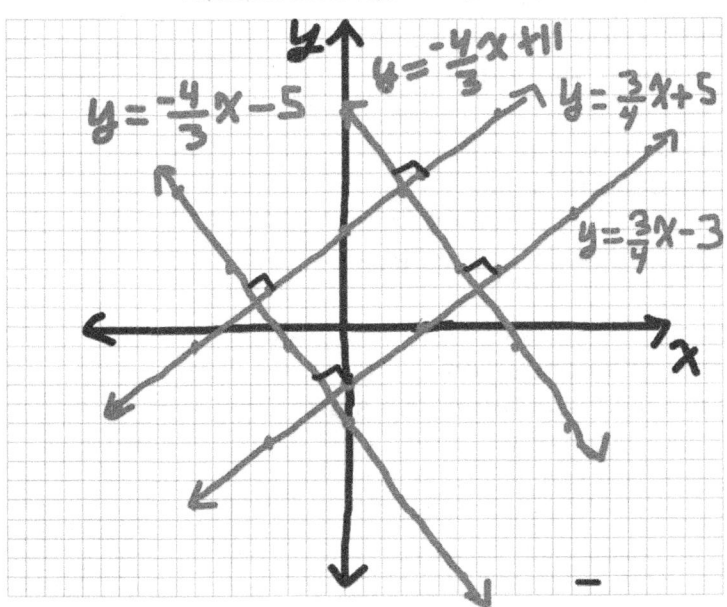

## Sequences & Series

Ducks in a row or dominos
A sequence makes me wonder
Line them up and let them go
They fall down by the number

A list of numbers, a particular rule
From one term to the next
What it's called, we learn in school
Put "Sequence" in the text

Take the sum, yes, add them up
The sequence of the numbers
Now call it a Series, that's what's up
We do this without wonder!

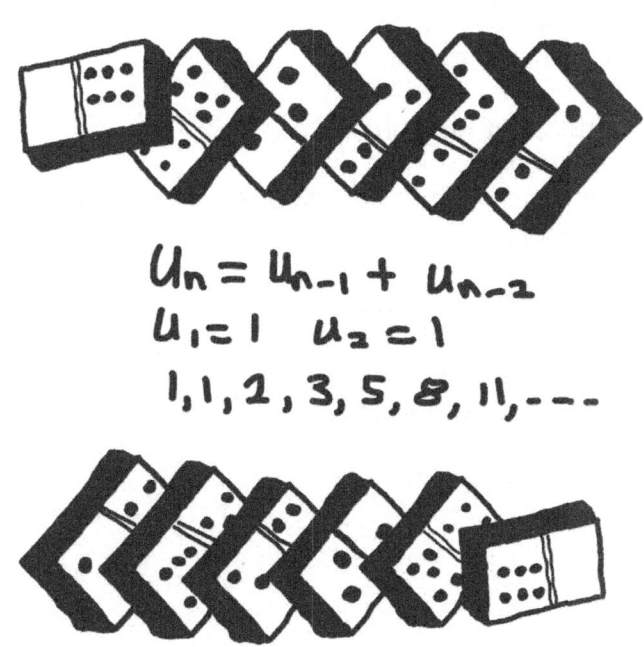

$$U_n = U_{n-1} + U_{n-2}$$
$$U_1 = 1 \quad U_2 = 1$$
$$1, 1, 2, 3, 5, 8, 11, \ldots$$

# Arithmetic Sequences and Series

A constant up or constant down
This sequence has a rule
A constant difference comes around
Today we learn in school

Arithmetic is what we call
The sequence with this pattern
The constant difference says it all
It's all that really matters

The constant difference, call it d
This is how it's found
Just subtract the term before you'll see
And then you write it down

The nth term formula you will need
Just multiply n minus 1
Times the constant we call d
Plus the first term just for fun

Arithmetic series, get the sum
A formula, really cool
It's n over 2, times the first and last one
A really useful tool

Arithmetic sequences, series too
I going to have to warn ya
It'll be a much easier time for you
If you memorize all the formulas

$$u_n = u_1 + (n-1)d$$
$$S_n = \frac{n}{2}(u_1 + u_n)$$
or
$$S_n = \frac{n}{2}(2u_1 + (n-1)d)$$

Ex:
$$3 + 6 + 9 + \cdots + 99$$
$$n = 33 \quad u_1 = 3$$
$$S_{33} = \frac{33}{2}(3+99) = 33(51)$$
$$= 1683$$

26

# Geometric Sequences & Series

2, 4, 8, 16
This sequence of four numbers
With constant multiplier look and see
It has to make you wonder

Geometric is what we call
This sequence, this is why
Its common ratio says it all
By the previous term divide

An nth term formula, its exponent see
It's r to the n minus 1
Times the first term, look and see
You'll find the very right one

Next we talk about a series
And sum up all the terms
A formula helps us do this clearly
It's something you can learn

Take 1 minus r to the power of n
And multiply by the first term
Divide by 1 minus r and then
The sum you have in turn

So find a term or take a sum
It's something that we do
Get this down and tell someone
All that you learned in school!

$$U_n = U_1 r^{n-1}$$

$$S_n = \frac{U_1(1-r^n)}{1-r}$$

$$S_\infty = \frac{U_1}{1-r} \quad 0 < |r| < 1$$

Ex: 3, 6, 12, 24 ...
$U_1 = 3 \quad r = 2 \quad U_5 = 3(2)^{5-1} = 48$

27

## Inverse Functions

Caterpillars change to butterflies, I heard
A function of natural fact
But changing back would be absurd
An inverse does just that

Output and input are interchanged
An inverse brings us back
To the input the function changed
An inverse function fact

To find an inverse, what we do
Is interchange y and x
Then solve for y and simplify too
With inverse notation next

A reflection of the function's graph
Across y equals x
The inverse function, I thought you asked
Is what is up there next

Butterflies going back in time
An inverse function's task
A caterpillar back to the starting line
To something from the past

# Function Combinations

Multiply, divide, add or subtract
Our functions f and g
Combined as one and left intact
It's easy as one, two, three

Add or subtract, combine like terms
With function combinations
Now one function with less concern
You'll have time for that vacation

Sometimes we multiply or maybe divide
Not trying to be a jerk
So don't forget the domain cries
Our input numbers work!


# Functions Review

Time to review the function's unit
It's what we do in school
We must retain the knowledge from it
And remember all the rules

Yes we want to go to college
Accomplish many goals
We must reactivate our knowledge
That's just the way it goes

For every input just one out
A function's what it's called
We sketch the graph and figure out
The line tests tells it all

An inverse function brings us back
From output back to in
It interchanges, that's a fact
Domain and range within

For compositions, a function in
Yes, to another function
With some effort and practicing
You'll do this by the luncheon

For transformations of functions too
Know how to plot the graph
The domain and range are there for you
I need to tell you that

A little practice is all you need
To master function facts
With some time you'll have the speed
And sleekness of a cat!

Evaluate the function for the different
input values: x = 2, -3, w, and t + 1.

$$f(x) = x^2 + 1$$

$f(2) = 2^2 + 1 = 5$

$f(-3) = (-3)^2 + 1 = 10$

$f(w) = w^2 + 1$

$f(t + 1) = (t + 1)^2 + 1$

$= (t + 1)(t + 1) + 1$

$= t^2 + t + t + 1 + 1$

$= t^2 + 2t + 2$

# Compound Interest

I put some money in the bank
The next thing that I knew
Compound interest made me thank
The day that I withdrew

The number of periods in a year
Please learn them all the same
So listen carefully, do not fear
We now present the names

Once a year means annually
Semi-annual means twice
Four times a year is quarterly
And monthly 12 is nice

Then there's daily 3-6-5
The number of days per year
We compound daily to survive
We have to make this clear

Last continuous seems so weird
Compounded infinitely
An easy formula stops the fear
You'll need to try and see!

Formula for Compound Interest

$$A = P\left(1 + \frac{r}{n}\right)^{nt}$$

$P =$ Principal Amount of Investment.

$r =$ Yearly rate of interest.

$t =$ Time in years.

$n =$ The number of compounding periods in a year.

## X-Y Intercepts

A graphical sketch must include
All the x and y intercepts
An intercept table helps you too
For finding where they are at

An x-intercept, where y equals zero
Just substitute zero for y
The y-intercept is when x equals zero
Please make sure you understand why

So plot the intercepts, sketch the graph
There is no need for you to worry
Just substitute zero you'll find them fast
Then write them on down in a hurry!

## Factoring

Sometimes when you factor in
The variables of this life
To overcome from where you've been
Brings everything to the light

Sometimes in math, we factor too
We find out what was multiplied
To get an expression, or number for you
And sometimes it helps us divide

Variables of life can factor in
It's something that is true
Just don't forget from where you've been
And learn how to factor too

# The Greatest Common Factor

A greatest factor in common with all
Those terms inside the expression
The GCF is what it's called
We'll learn today in the lesson

When you factor, look for this first
The common factor throughout
The distributive property used in reverse
Will help you to factor it out

Oh GCF, My BFF
Please help me to do my best
I need to factor until nothing's left
To help prepare for the test

## FOIL: First, Inside, Outside, Last

$(3x-1)(2x+7)$

$6X^2 + 21x - 2x - 7$

$6x^2 + 19x - 7$

General Distribution: Take each term from the first
polynomial, and distribute it to the second. Finish
by collecting like terms and simplifying.

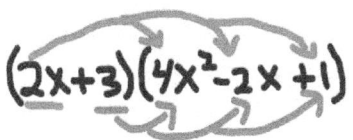

$(2x+3)(4x^2-2x+1)$

$8x^3 - 4x^2 + 2x + 12x^2 - 6x + 3$

$8x^3 + 8x^2 - 4x + 3$

# Factoring Trinomials

It's better to practice how to factor
I heard in a testimonial
There is no need to be an actor
When factoring a trinomial

A pair of binomials multiplied
Into a trinomial expression
These are the factors that coincide
You'll learn about in this lesson

First times first gives first in the tri
Choose factors that make this true
Last times last is also applied
For the last term in the tri too

Don't forget to double-check
The middle term is why
The O and I combine to this
For factors of the tri

Trial and error, yes it is
When choosing the right factors
A little practice makes you a wiz
No need to be an actor

$$(2x + 3)(x - 2)$$

$$3x$$
$$-4x$$
$$-x$$

$$2x^2 - 1x - 6$$

FF    O+I    LL

Trinomial factoring is the inverse of
binomial multiplication. The object is
to find the pair of binomials that
multiply together to give the trinomial.

Notice that when we multiply two binomials
into a trinomial, the O and I from FOIL
combine to the middle term of the trinomial.

Ex:  $x^2 + 5x + 6$

$(x + 3)(x + 2)$

34

# Exponential Functions

Certain functions are mathematically essential
For modeling growth and decay
We call these functions exponential
They're what we'll learn today

The input is an exponent
That's how it gets its name
Exponential functions meant
The growth might be insane

The standard equation read the text
We learn this on the fly
It's y equals 'a' times 'b' to the 'x'
You just have to give it a try

When b is a number greater than 1
It's time to talk about growth
But if it goes between zero and 1
Decay's what we put in the notes

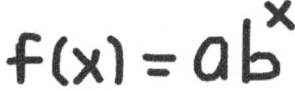

$$f(x) = ab^x$$

Where 'a' is the y-intercept, an b is the multiplier.

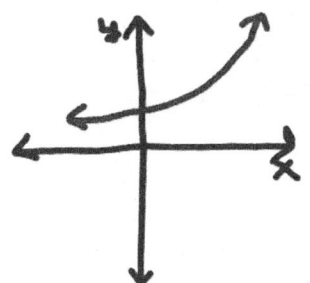
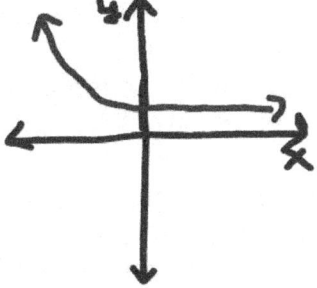

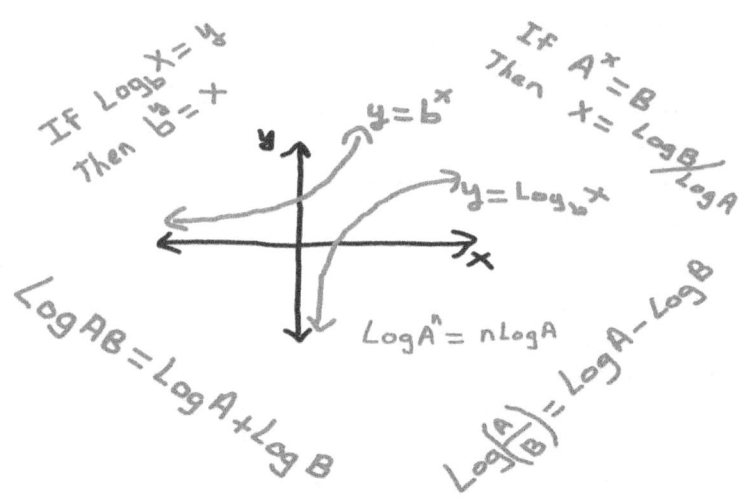

If $\log_b x = y$
Then $b^y = x$

$y = b^x$

$y = \log_b x$

If $A^x = B$
Then $x = \dfrac{\log B}{\log A}$

$\log A^n = n \log A$

$\log AB = \log A + \log B$

$\log\left(\dfrac{A}{B}\right) = \log A - \log B$

## An Exponential's Inverse

An exponential function's inverse
In math we call it a log
It's not so bad, so please rehearse
To keep your brain out of the fog

The exponential's base, call it b
It's also the logarithm's base
It will help you convert it accurately
From one form to another in case

Its graph is an exponential's reflection
Over the line y equals x
Domain and range in case you are checking
Will interchange like all the rest

For solving exponential equations
We now can use our logs
With some practice and a little persuasion
You'll keep your brain out of the fog

# Properties of Logs

I bet you thought you had some rhythm
You thought you had a clue
About the properties of logarithms
In math we have a few

A useful property when you have it
We call the sum of logs
Turns into the log of a product
Please write this in your blog

The difference of logs, a property too
Is now the log of a quotient
The log of a single argument through
Will help at the critical moment

The exponent of the argument next
Moves out in front of the log
Now a multiple, read the text
I hope this lift the fog


# Logarithmic Functions

Linear functions are simply straight lines
Quadratics the shape of a U
Exponential growth, a steep incline
And through the roof it grew!

Then Logarithmic came around
An inverse exponential
The exponent now can be brought down
Log functions are essential

Our trusty logs they have a base
Exponentials have one too
It just so happens to be the case
They're both the same, it's true

The input is the argument
An Exponent it does equal
A base called b, so what this meant
That converting's our next sequel

Base to the power of the exponent
Equals the argument
Another form converted in
Exponential form its now in!

## Exponential Equations

Equation solving in math is essential
You just have to learn the steps
Time to learn to solve exponentials
With practice you'll learn like the rest

The inverse cancels all components
An exponent is all that's left
When solving for the exponent
A log can help with that

So isolate the base and exponent too
All by itself to one side
Then take the log and cancel it through
The exponent's all that abides

There is a shortcut that we do
When 'b' to the 'x' is 'a'
It's log of 'a' over log of 'b' too
And It equals 'x', all day!

# Quadratic Form Exponential

A substitution helps you through
Some exponential equations
It turns into a quadratic too
A very special occasion

Just solve the quadratic normally
And back substitute when through
You now can solve it more easily
Quadratics are something we do

Exponentials in quadratic form
In math it's nothing new
A little practice will help you perform
The steps to get you through

# Logarithmic Equations

Math is great, it's logical too
And sometimes helps solve arguments
Logarithmic properties are there for you
When solving a logarithmic argument!

Condense the logs, combine together
Down to a single term
A single log is so much better
Much less to be concerned

The argument now, is easy to solve
Just convert to exponent form
A single argument is now involved
From here the solution is born

Don't forget to check solutions
Extraneous ones we forget
Discard those ones that cause confusion
Keep those in the domain yet!

# Graphing Exponential Functions

A pattern of growth, or maybe decay
It's time that we take notes
We see its graph, it's on display
Exponentials are the GOAT!

Exponential growth, it has a pattern
Continually curving up
We reach so high, we get to Saturn
Exponential is enough

Then decay, we say no way
To exponential loss
But please don't worry, it's okay
You get to be the boss!

Just shift it left, or shift it right
Remember transformations?
If you do, you'll win the fight
For graphing that equation

Show your friends, it's so essential
In math it's what we do
Display your skills in exponentials
The world will sure love you!

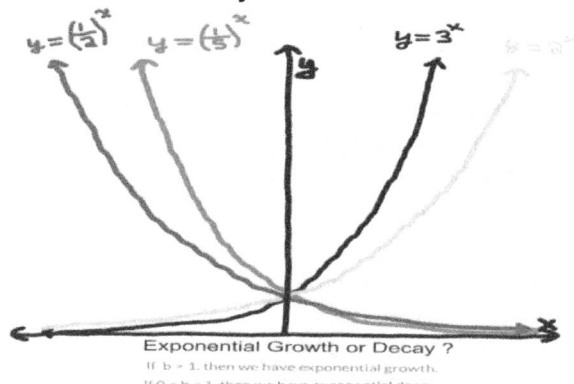

Exponential Growth or Decay ?
If b > 1, then we have exponential growth.
If 0 < b < 1, then we have exponential decay.

# Right Triangle Trig

A right triangle here or another one there
They're everywhere you look
Construction sites or grandpa's chair
They're even in some books

We need some math to help us out
To find those angles and sides
Math of triangles without a doubt
Should come as no surprise

Opposite, adjacent, hypotenuse
Please know about these sides
They're relative to the angle used
And make you sound so wise

SOH-CAH-TOA, a mnemonic device
For memorizing trig
Just say it once or maybe twice
It really helps you big

The sine of an angle, heard the news
Remember it's the SOH
It's opposite over the hypotenuse
The very first ratio

Cosine's fine, looks like sine
Remember using CAH
The adjacent over the hypotenuse line
And it even has a law

Using TOA, off on a tangent
Slope or steepness of lines
Opposite over adjacent imagine
Would help almost all of the time

Right triangle trig, let's think big
Let's solve for sides or angles
Indirect measure, is our next gig
The math of right triangles!

# SOH-CAH-TOA

$$\text{Sin}\,\theta = \frac{\text{OPP}}{\text{HYP}} \quad \text{Cos}\,\theta = \frac{\text{Adj}}{\text{HYP}} \quad \text{Tan}\,\theta = \frac{\text{OPP}}{\text{Adj}}$$

$$\text{Sin}\,A = \frac{a}{c} \qquad \text{Sin}\,B = \frac{b}{c}$$

$$\text{Cos}\,A = \frac{b}{c} \qquad \text{Cos}\,B = \frac{a}{c}$$

$$\text{Tan}\,A = \frac{a}{b} \qquad \text{Tan}\,B = \frac{b}{a}$$

# The Six Trig Ratios

Sine, Cosine, and Tangent please
SOH-CAH-TOA a mnemonic device
A nifty way to memorize these
Three trig ratios come out nice

Now with three trig ratios
We take reciprocals
We now have six trig ratios
That's just the way it goes

Cosecant, Secant, and Cotangent
Reciprocals of the three
Sine, Cosine and Tangent
Will help remember these

Cosecant and Sine, Secant and Cosine
No two Co's go together
Cotangent and Tangent are by design
Reciprocals to the letter

## Reciprocal Trig Ratios

$$Sin\theta = \frac{1}{csc\theta} \qquad Cos\theta = \frac{1}{Sec\theta} \qquad Tan\theta = \frac{1}{Cot\theta}$$

$$Sin\theta = \frac{O}{H} \qquad Csc\theta = \frac{H}{O}$$

$$Cos\theta = \frac{A}{H} \qquad Sec\theta = \frac{H}{A}$$

$$Tan\theta = \frac{O}{A} \qquad Cot\theta = \frac{A}{O}$$

## Angle of Rotation

A starting ray, rotate around
A direction counterclockwise
A positive angle, write it down
The quadrant where it resides

The initial side, it all begins
With angles of rotation
The terminal side it surely ends
Make sure you use notation

Clockwise angles, nothing personal
Negative! We label these
It helps keep track of the way to go
Or the direction of the breeze

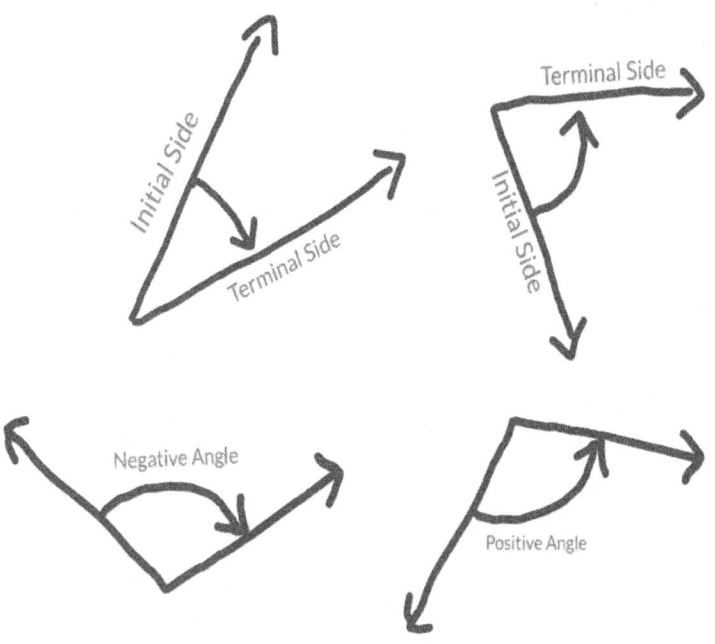

# Standard Position Angles

The x and y coordinate system
We place our angle there
Standard form will help precision
When doing trig with care

The initial side, the positive x
With quadrants one through four
The terminal side we read the text
Will get you in the door

Positive or negative also applies
According to direction
Negative angles go clockwise
We learn it in this section

Angles put in standard form
Will help us do our trig
Any angle will conform
It matters not how big

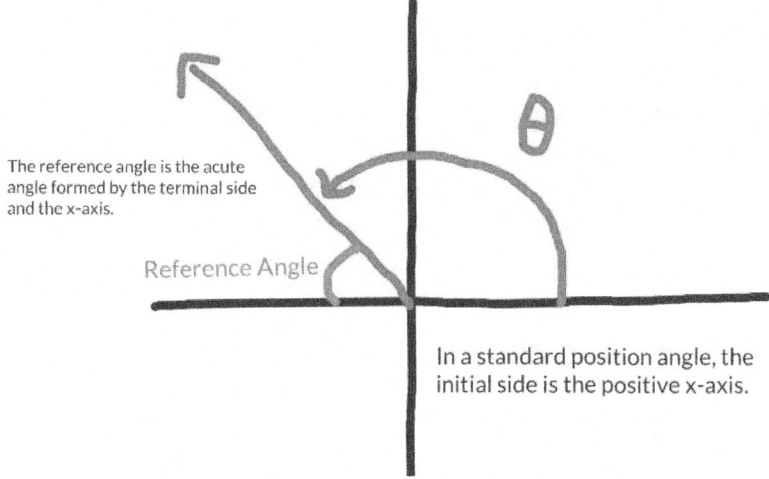

The reference angle is the acute angle formed by the terminal side and the x-axis.

Reference Angle

In a standard position angle, the initial side is the positive x-axis.

# Reference Angles

An acute angle formed by the terminal side
Along with the x-axis
The reference angle there abides
For trig we will enact this

A reference triangle we can form
From the reference angle
All trig ratios now are born
You'll write them when you go

Positive or negative legs by direction
A positive hypotenuse
Pythagoras helps, no need for guessing
We don't have much to lose

# Coterminal Angles

Different angles with terminal sides
Identically the same
The same trig values must abide
Coterminal is the name

Their reference angles coincide
It helps us to think big
Write them down and start the ride
It's time to do some trig

CoTerminal Angles

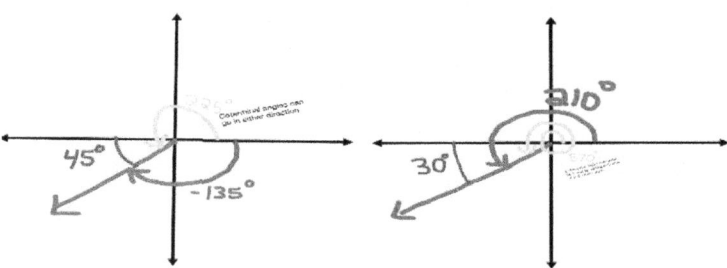

# Trig of any Angle

Angles between zero and ninety degrees
Every right triangle has two
But what about angles greater than these?
What kind of trig can you do?

Standard form, please sketch the angle
Reference triangle include
Do the trig and don't get tangled
The ratios can be negative too

All Students Take Calculus, ASTC
To remember the trig functions' sign
A positive or negative function you'll see
Depends on the quadrant it lies

# Radians & Degrees

An angle of rotation, all the way around
Equals 360 degrees
A unit of measure we have found
For measuring angles, you see

With length, so many different measures
Like miles, inches or feet
Also with angles are units to consider
Like radians which make math neat

Now when the circle's arc length measure
Equals the radius too
A single radian we can treasure
Two pi's when we rotate through

360 incremental degrees
Equals two pi radians
A formula for converting these
Will help whatever stage you're in

One-eighty over pi, we multiply
When converting to degrees
The conversion formula must apply
With practice it's a breeze

Pi over one-eighty, we multiply
A conversion into radians
And don't forget to leave the pi
Our decimals don't work great at this

Different units of angle measure
Like radians and degrees
With some practice, know for sure
You'll get through this with ease

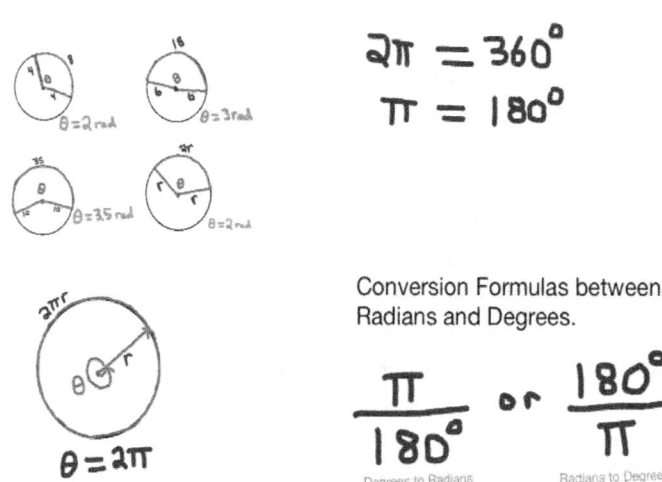

$$2\pi = 360^{\circ}$$
$$\pi = 180^{\circ}$$

Conversion Formulas between Radians and Degrees.

$$\frac{\pi}{180^{\circ}} \quad or \quad \frac{180^{\circ}}{\pi}$$

Degrees to Radians          Radians to Degrees

# Unit Circle

A circle with radius equal to one
The unit circle it is called
It helps with trig, to get it done
To understand it all

The point where the terminal side goes through
The trig values there reside
They're on the circle, you'll find them too
You just need the x and the y

x is cosine, y is the sine
No matter what angle size
Tangent is y over x all the time
From the point on the terminal side

Now angles in multiples of 90 degrees
Or angles from special right tri's
The circle we'll help us do trig with ease
With no calculator you can get by

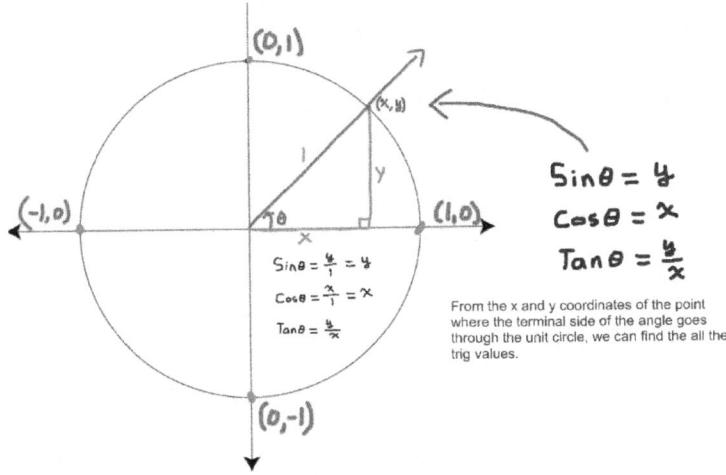

From the x and y coordinates of the point where the terminal side of the angle goes through the unit circle, we can find the all the trig values.

49

# Special Right Triangles

Something special without doubt
With certain types of angles
You can work it out without
Calculators or trig tables

Special triangles we can make
When using special angles
The unknown sides, a piece of cake
You'll find all six trig ratios

Isosceles Right, we call this special
With legs congruent too
The hypotenuse is nothing monumental
It's the leg times the square root of two

Thirty-sixty-ninety, we call this special
With a long and a short leg too
Hypotenuse found right from the get go
Just multiply the short leg by two

The short leg times square root of three
Gives the leg that's long
This helps do trig precise you'll see
And maybe sing a song

## Special Right

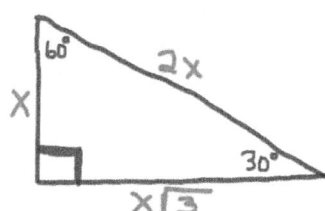 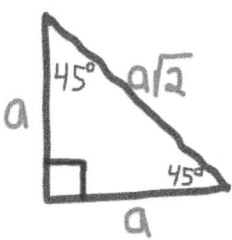

50

## Point on the Terminal Side

A point on the angle's terminal side
We'd like to do some trig
A reference triangle from the point abides
From there we will think big

Positive or negative, the triangle's legs
According to the point
The x-y values give it away
It surely is the point

Hypotenuse positive? It's always true
The legs are always squared
A bit of advice from Pythagoras too
We'll write it down with care

With reference triangle now in place
We now can do our trig
All six ratios just in case
It's really nothing big

The point (-5,12) lies on the terminal side of
an angle, find the value of the six trig ratios.

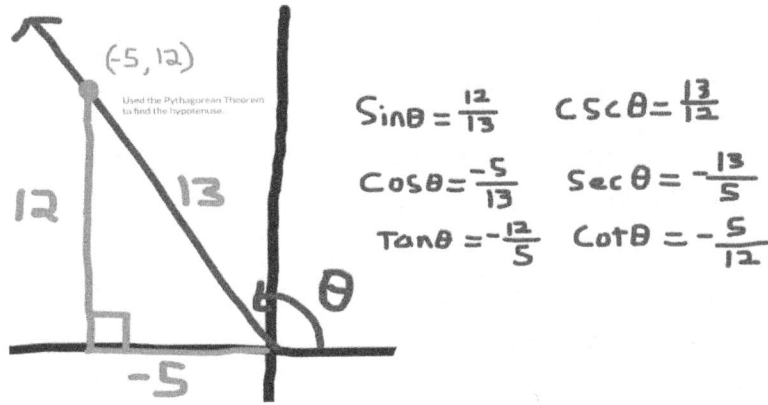

$$Sin\theta = \frac{12}{13} \qquad csc\theta = \frac{13}{12}$$

$$Cos\theta = \frac{-5}{13} \qquad Sec\theta = -\frac{13}{5}$$

$$Tan\theta = -\frac{12}{5} \qquad Cot\theta = -\frac{5}{12}$$

# Graph of Sine and Cosine

Periodic functions, sine and cosine
We learn them when we do trig
Let us graph them; it's done all the time
It's really nothing big

The unit circle, the parent's friend
With quarter increments around
Sine and cosine, you'll find it when
The x's and y's are found

Around and around the circle we go
A 360 degree cycle
It's called the period, well what do you know
Your teacher's name is Michael

When using radians, please don't sneeze
The period's equal two pi
It's just like 360 degrees
Around the circle is why

Divide 360 or two pi
By dilation factor, b
The transformed period's the reason why
You'll find it easily

The horizontal scale, next we find
It's the period divided by four
For graphing sine or even cosine
You'll need it even more

Next is amplitude you make the call
It's just a vertical dilation
Multiply the function; that is all
Then go on that vacation

The vertical shift or horizontal axis
They both are one in the same
It's up or down like paying taxes
Sinusoidal's the name of the game

Last horizontal phase displacement
Oh what the heck is this?
Horizontal translation, what it meant
I think we get the gist

Now to put it all together
To sketch the graph you'll see
Know the alphabetic letters
a, b, c and d

The middle axis of the plot
A dashed line using "d"
Begins the sketch, so ready or not
You'll do this part with ease

The amplitude, we call it "a"
The distance from the center
Above or below what can I say?
The max or the min we enter

Next is "c," it's where it starts
Mark it on the axis
Add the scale, the next part
You'll master this with practice

Now start the sketch according to
The sine or cosine pattern
It's really easy all you do
Is sketch it like it matters!

Middle-Max-Middle-Min
A pattern to unwind
We call it sine it's not a sin
A pattern so divine

Max-Middle-Min-Middle
The pattern of cosine
Just kick back and play the fiddle
You'll sketch the graph just fine

$$f(\theta) = a\sin(b(\theta - c)) + d$$

$$f(\theta) = 3\sin(2(\theta - 10)) + 1$$

$$a = 3 \quad c = 10$$
$$b = 2 \quad d = 1$$
$$P = \frac{360}{2} = 180°$$
$$H_{sc1.} = \frac{180}{4} = 45°$$

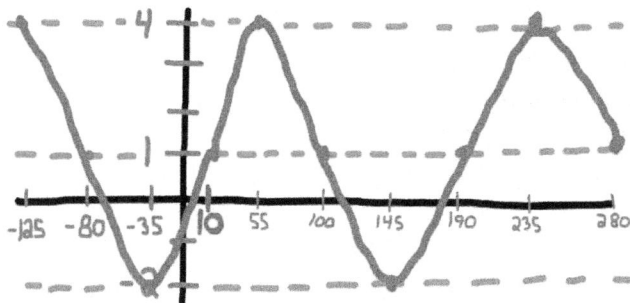

"a" the amplitude, is the distance from the middle to either the max or min of the graph. "b" is used for finding the period, and horizontal scale. "c" is the horizontal shift (the start of the graph), and "d" is the location of the sinusoidal axis (middle of graph).

## Solving Trig Equations

We solved equations of many kinds
It's time we now think big
Yes, I think it's now the time
For solving ones with trig

We take the sine or cosine too
Or sometimes just the tangent
For trig equations it's what we do
It's just what we imagined

Isolate the function to one side
Our normal steps will do
The equation now is simplified
Some trig will help us through

First find the quadrant, 1 to 4
All Students will Take Calculus
ASTC, that's what it's for
The sign will help us out with this

A reference angle with inverse trig
It's what we should find next
Please put it down, it's nothing big
It's even on the test!

Multiples of 360 or maybe $2\pi$
Solutions may be infinite
The period of sine or cosine's why
Just believe and you can do it

$$\text{Sin}\theta = \frac{-\sqrt{3}}{2}$$

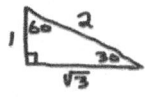

The reference angle is 60°, and the sine is negative in quadrants 3 and 4.

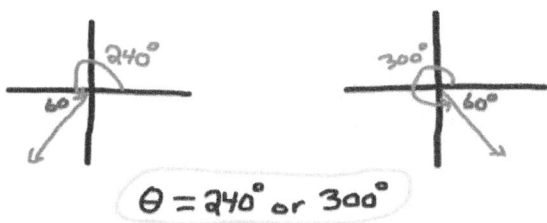

$$\theta = 240° \text{ or } 300°$$

## The Law of Sines

A universe governed by rules and laws
Existence in space and time
Triangle rules are part of the clause
They follow the Law of Sines!

Sine of the angle, to its opposite side
Will always be the same
No matter which angle or side you try
The ratio is part of the game

The reciprocal law is also applied
The side to the sine of an angle
For finding unknown angles or sides
On any kind of triangle!

When to use the Law of Sines?
Just look to what is shown
An angle to its opposite side
Is something that is known

All Triangles must follow the Law!

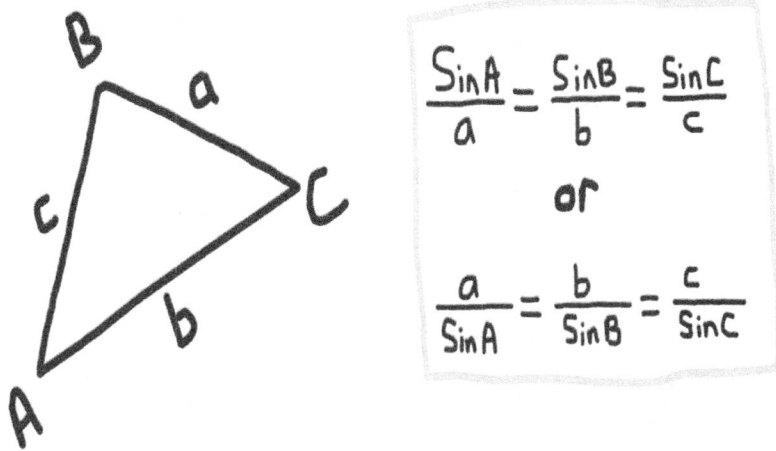

$$\frac{Sin A}{a} = \frac{Sin B}{b} = \frac{Sin C}{c}$$

or

$$\frac{a}{Sin A} = \frac{b}{Sin B} = \frac{c}{Sin C}$$

For any particular triangle, the Sine of an angle divided by the length of the opposite side is always the same.

## Law of Cosines

It's on the books, another law
Triangles, must obey
The Law of Cosine's in the clause
There's nothing they can say

The sum of the squares of a and b
Minus two ab cosine C
Gives 'c' squared accordingly
They follow the law you can see

The Pythagorean Theorem in disguise
If angle C is right
Cosine's zero to the wise
It drops right out of sight

Oh Pythagoras thought really big
But this he never saw
If he only knew his trig
He may have known the law!

# Law of Cosines

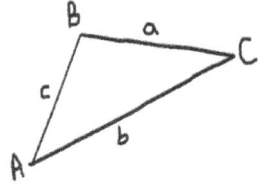

$$a^2 = b^2 + c^2 - 2bc\cos A$$

$$b^2 = a^2 + c^2 - 2ac\cos B$$

$$c^2 = a^2 + b^2 - 2ab\cos C$$

$$\cos A = \frac{b^2 + c^2 - a^2}{2bc}$$

$$\cos B = \frac{a^2 + c^2 - b^2}{2ac}$$

$$\cos C = \frac{a^2 + b^2 - c^2}{2ab}$$

**Ex:**

$$c^2 = 6^2 + 8^2 - 2(6)(8)\cos(20°)$$

$$c^2 \approx 9.79$$

$$c \approx 3.13$$

# The Sky is the Limit

The sky's the limit, you've heard them say
Please go out and tell everyone
You can do more than you thought in a day
And still have time for some fun

So it's time to put your minds at ease
And think about some goals
Let's think about limits mathematically
Where does that function go?

Approaches a number from the left
The same one from the right
When this happens, what is next?
A limit is in sight!

Continuous function at a number
This is what to do
Substitute in, no need to wonder
The limit's there for you

Discontinuous, out of the domain
It doesn't mean you're through
Just rewrite, don't go insane
Then try to substitute

When you truly hit your limit
This is how you'll know
You've reached the sky with no bounds in it
Because every day you grow!

$$\lim_{x \to 1}\left(\frac{x^3 - 1}{x - 1}\right) = \lim_{x \to 1}(x^2 + x + 1)$$

note: $\frac{x^2 - 1}{x - 1} = \frac{(x-1)(x^2 + x + 1)}{(x-1)} = x^2 + x + 1$

$$\lim_{x \to 1}(x^2 + x + 1) = 1^2 + 1 + 1 = 3$$

The graph below has what we call a hole at x = 1, this is because x cannot equal 1. However, the graph approaches the value of 3 when x approaches 1. Therefore, the limit as x approaches 1 equals 3.

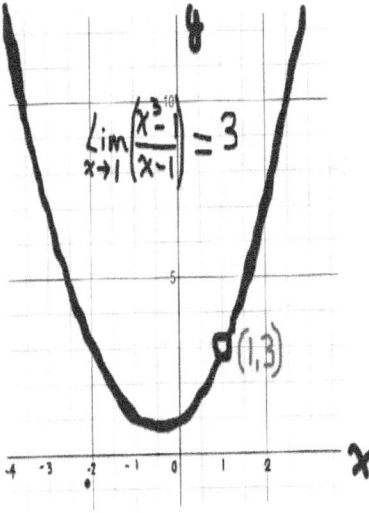

$$\lim_{x \to 1}\left(\frac{x^3 - 1}{x - 1}\right) = 3$$

(1,3)

# The Derivative

The rate of change of a point on a curve
The slope of a tangent line
Taking the derivative will find this I heard
Something we do all the time

First, we take f of x plus h
Then subtract f of x
Divide this all again by h
Then set up the limit next

The slope of the secant line we get
Before we take the limit
As h approaches zero yet
The slope of the tangent is in it

A continuous function's rate of change
A derivative's all you need
Tangent lines are not so strange
Their slope can always be seen!

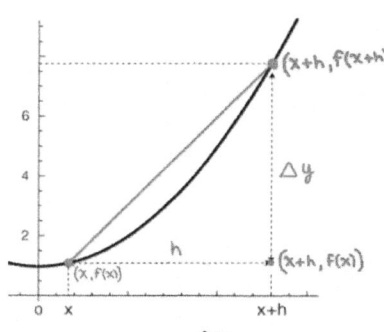

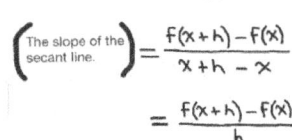

$$(\text{Slope}) = \frac{\Delta y}{h}$$

$$\left(\begin{array}{l}\text{The slope of the}\\\text{secant line.}\end{array}\right) = \frac{f(x+h) - f(x)}{x+h - x}$$

$$= \frac{f(x+h) - f(x)}{h}$$

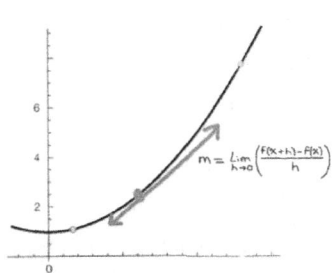

As h approaches 0, the secant line becomes a tangent line. The derivative gives the slope of the tangent line at a point along the curve.

# The Power Rule

The limit definition, with f of x plus h
Was great for intuition
But it surely made my forearm ache
So we need something more efficient

The power rule for x to the n
Subtract one from the exponent
Multiply by n, and what you have then
The derivative right at the moment

Polynomial functions of many terms
Differentiate one by one
The power rule is not a concern
It's easy and it's fun

For linear functions please take note
I know this may sound strange
The derivative here is just the slope
The constant rate of change

Horizontal lines are constant terms
They have a slope of zero
A constant's derivative is no concern
Because it also equals zero

So goodbye limit definition
Goodbye achy arm
The Power Rule's coming in
It works just like a charm!

## The Product Rule

Any two functions can be multiplied
Before we differentiate
And one thing we know when we simplify
Is the power rule works really great

But there's really no reason to multiply
Before differentiating
The Product Rule's the reason why
You won't have to keep your friends waiting

Its f prime g plus f-g prime
It's all you have to do
People do this all the time
When they take math in high school


## The Quotient Rule

A quotient of functions, f over g
You could try long division
And then differentiate carefully
But you could make another decision

The Quotient Rule for derivatives
For the quotient of f and g
No long division required for this
Just follow the steps and you'll see

f prime g minus f-g prime
All of this put over
The function g squared all the time
The derivative's what's leftover

With the Quotient Rule, there's no divide
With functions f and g
For rational functions this rule applies
To differentiate easily

$$f'(x) = \lim_{h \to 0} \frac{f(x+h) - f(x)}{h}$$

$$\frac{d}{dx}\left(x^n\right) = nx^{n-1}$$

$$(f \pm g)'(x) = f'(x) \pm g'(x)$$

$$(af(x))' = af'(x)$$

# The Chain Rule

A ball and chain, it seems so now
But persistence sets the sail
Do your homework, do it proud
And soon you will prevail

A composite function's derivative
It's not a ball and chain
Anyone with initiative
Will not rack their brains

The Chain Rule for derivatives
Will help to keep you sane
Time to now get rid of it
It's time to break the chains

The outsides function's derivative
Times the inside derivative too
Something for the inquisitive
The derivative is found for you

So break the chains that hold us back
And do your work each day
Our trusty Chain Rule helps with that
It's math; what can I say?

$$(fg)' = f'g + fg'$$

$$(F(g(x)))' = f'(g(x)) \cdot g'(x)$$

$$\left(\frac{f}{g}\right)' = \frac{f'g - fg'}{g^2}$$

# Higher Order Derivatives

Take the derivative over again
The second derivative you get
Take it again, and what you have then
The third derivative you can bet

Take the derivative again and again
You've now reached the higher order
A fourth or a fifth derivative then
You'll be called a derivative hoarder!

$$E_x: \quad f = 3x^4 - 2x^3$$

$$f' = 12x^3 - 6x^2$$

$$f'' = 36x^2 - 12x$$

$$f''' = 72x - 12$$

$$f^{(4)} = 72$$

To compute a higher order derivative, just differentiate over and over again.

# Notation

The letter **s** stands for the position, **v** means velocity, and **a** is for acceleration.

 $s(t)$

Position, at time t, I write a lower case s to avoid confusion with the number 5.

$v(t)$

Velocity at time t.

$a(t)$

Acceleration at time t.

$s'(t) = v(t)$

The derivative of the position of something is its velocity.

$s''(t) = v'(t) = a(t)$

The derivative of velocity is the acceleration. Notice that acceleration is also the second derivative of position.

66

# Trig Differentiation

Sine, cosine and tangent, please
You know they're functions too
One thing you can do with ease
Is differentiate them on cue

The derivative of sine is just cosine
And cosines derivative is the negative sine
It's something you can do all the time
While taking the derivative of cosine and sine

With tangent's derivative don't be scared
Because it's really nothing new
It's equal to the secant squared
That's all you have to do

Something important to think about
The Chain Rule here applies
The inside derivative don't leave out
It must be multiplied

$$\frac{d}{dx}\left(\sin x\right) = \cos x$$

$$\frac{d}{dx}\left(\cos x\right) = -\sin x$$

$$\frac{d}{dx}\left(\tan x\right) = \sec^2 x$$

# Derivative of e to the x

The exponential is what it's called
A function we sometimes need
The base of the natural log is all
We call it a function indeed

A base of e, an exponent x
It's the easiest one we'll see
Differentiate the function! Read the text
You'll be done before counting to three

Its derivative simply equals itself
Times the derivative of its exponent
You can do it, all by yourself
It's the easiest one at the moment


# Differentiating the Natural Log

There's no need to be in the fog
When the base of the log is natural
To differentiate this log
Just follow the steps and be factual

You take the argument's derivative
And then you multiply
By one over what's inside of it
The argument to the wise

So now that you are out of the fog
With natural log derivatives
It's time to stop and take a pause
From here it's your initiative

# Extreme Values

My relative Max and relative Min
In valleys or hilltops they live
The derivative locates all of them
The critical numbers it gives

On a closed interval, Max and Min
They surely both reside there
Totally extreme, as we've ever been
Critical numbers beware!

Test the endpoints, and critical numbers
Into the function, you see
Max and Min will make us wonder
How easy to find where they'll be


# Critical Numbers

My relative Max and relative Min
It's easy to find you all day
Up on a hilltop or valley within
The derivative gives you away

A horizontal tangent line
Where Max and Min reside
Or where the slope is undefined
You might find them inside

So set the derivative equal to zero
To find those critical numbers
Max and Min, you are my heroes
To anyone who wonders

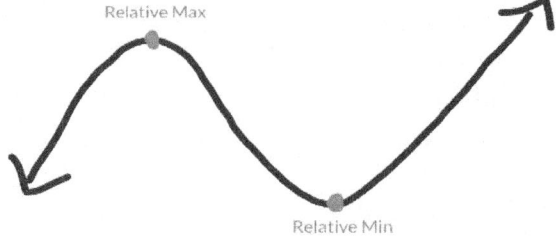

Relative Max

Relative Min

## The First Derivative Test

The first derivative test don't fear
It's nothing that you thought
Nothing to cram for let's be clear
A lesson that you're taught

Start by finding critical numbers
Then set up the open intervals
Min and Max in case you wondered
Are in valleys or up on a hill

Increasing to decreasing on a hilltop
Our relative Max resides
A critical number helps stay on top
Of where he'll try to hide

Decreasing to increasing in the valley
Our relative Min is down there
Critical numbers will help us tally
The precise location of where

Sometimes with our critical number
The sign, it does not change
Where is Max or Min, I wondered?
They're somewhere out of range

The derivative gives the rate of change at any point along a curve. The rate of change is measured by the slope of the tangent line at that point. The slope will change from positive to negative along a hilltop (max), and will go from negative to positive through a valley (min).

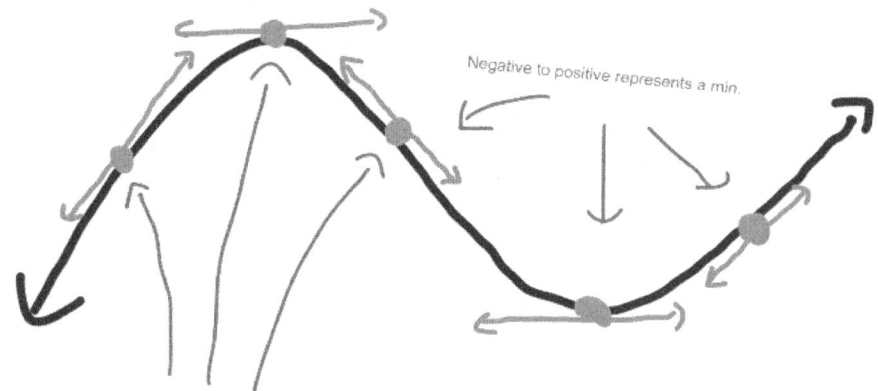

Negative to positive represents a min.

When the slope of the tangent line (derivative) goes from positive to negative, then the critical number is at the local max.

## Concavity

Oh Max, and Min, where have you been?
Quit hiding out from me
Up on a hilltop or valley within
You're out there, I can see

I'm an expert on concavity
It's either up or down
Therefore you can't hide from me
Or make me look like a clown

A derivative increasing, concave up
A valley down below
Our relative Min is in the cup
The lowest you can go

Derivative's decreasing, concave down
Way up on the hilltop
Our relative Max, he likes to clown
Sometimes I wish he'd stop

So with a negative 2nd derivative
The graph is concave down
Our relative Max, it's where he lives
The biggest man in town

A positive 2nd derivative yes
We now are concave up
Our relative Min is the best
She lives at the bottom of the cup

Point of inflection. Where concavity switches over.

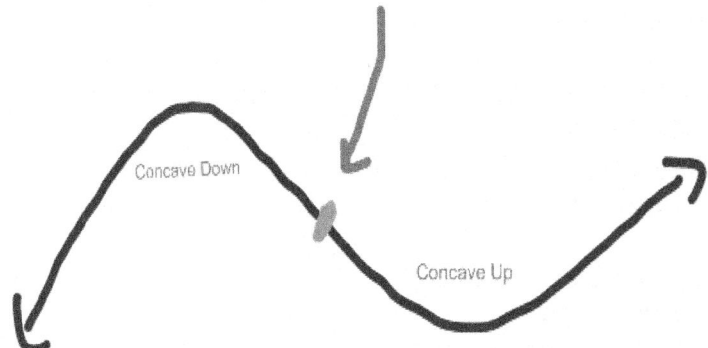

Concave Down

Concave Up

# 2nd Derivative Test

Max on the hilltop, Min in the valley
They're always so extreme
It's probably why my sister, Sally
Had to leave the scene

A second derivative test, I wondered
Extremes can't hide from me
Just substitute some critical numbers
This test will help you see

A positive output, concave up
Our Min is found down there
Our second derivative is enough
To find precisely where

Concave down, a negative test
Our Max lives on a hilltop
He's way above, and gives his best
And doesn't ever stop

If the output equals zero
The second test won't do
Back to the first test, here we go
It's nothing really new!

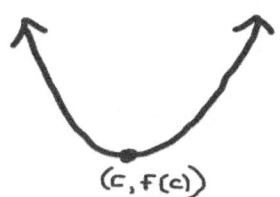

When the second derivative is positive, the graph is concave down, which makes the value at the critical number a minimum.

When the second derivative is negative, the graph is concave up, which makes the value at the critical number a maximum.

# Point of Inflection, POI

The point where concavity turns around
It's called a POI
A point of inflection makes no sound
Sometimes I wonder why

Point of Inflection, POI
A 2nd derivative's root
Concavity changes that is why
Mathematicians give a hoot

Critical number, 1st derivative
I have to make this clear
Roots of a function's 2nd derivative
Are never critical here

Determine the intervals where the graph is concave up or down, and give the point of inflection

$$y = x^4 - 4x^3$$

Possible POI's are roots of the second derivative.

$y' = 4x^3 - 12x^2$

$y'' = 12x^2 - 24x = 0$
$= 12x(x-2) = 0$
$x = 0 \text{ or } 2$

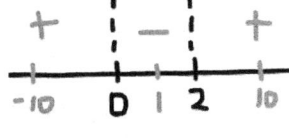

$(x<0)$ cc up

$(0<x<2)$ cc down

$(x>2)$ cc up

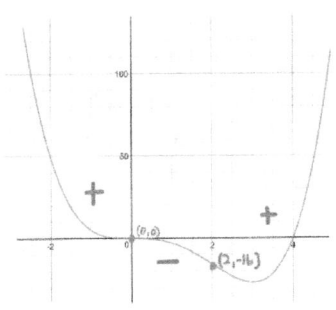

POI : $(0,0)$
$(2,-16)$

74

## Students Welcome!

Here we are back, face-to-face
It's been about a year
Welcome students to this place
I want that to be clear

To make this work, we must be safe
Three feet apart is fine
We wear a mask, it's just the case
It's where we draw the line

If you're DL, don't forget
You're part of our class too
Just keep the proper mindset yet
Until the year is through

If our tech shall let us down
And ruin our day's lesson
The recording of it can be found
On Schoology in its section

So to my students, welcome back!
Let's finish up this year
Just work hard, I've got your back
So now let's give a cheer!

# The AntiDerivative

It's over the horizon, I feel it near
A chill runs down my spine
The antiderivative is what we fear
It's just a matter of time

The sun is darkened, the moon blood red
Fire from the sky
The antiderivative bore its head
And students wept and cried

The book of mathematics was read aloud
Revealing the secret to life
The antiderivative fooled the crowd
About what is wrong or right

Right is wrong, wrong is right
Everyone was deceived
Confusion, divisions, sealed the plight
Because no one believed

Integrate at the trumpet sound
I heard a desperate plea
The antiderivative stood its ground
And students began to flee

Derivative undone, back to the start
To the original function too
The antiderivative did its part
So it won't come after you

Don't be deceived, it has other names
So time to start believing
You can do it, it's not a game
It's all about achieving

## The Definite Integral

Integrate the function from a to b
The Fundamental Theorem
Of calculus finds the area you'll see
These skills you're going to need them

Truly definite, yes indeed
The area beneath the curve
Between the x-axis from a to b
We'll find it, that's for sure

Take the antiderivative, call it F
It's something that you'll need
F of "b" minus F of "a" next
It's easy as 1-2-3

The area between the curve and x-axis
On the interval from "a" to "b"
Surely definite and precise like taxes
The area for you and for me

The area under the curve $x^2$ from x = 2 to x = 7

$$\int_{2}^{7} x^2\,dx = \left.\frac{x^3}{3}\right|_{2}^{7} = \frac{7^3}{3} - \frac{2^3}{3} = \frac{343}{3} - \frac{8}{3}$$

$$= \frac{335}{3} \text{ sq.units}$$

## U- Substitution

A composite function's antiderivative
The chain rule in reverse
It's something that is not intuitive
We really must rehearse

The inside function call it U
Please don't call it me
A simpler problem for you to do
When we substitute carefully

Substitute du for dx
It's something that we do
A derivative with respect to x
Will help to get us through

Integrate with respect to U
And don't forget the C
Back substitute and then you're through
With practice you will see

## Integrating the Exponential Function

An exponential function, e to the x
The derivative equals itself
The antiderivative is what's up next
You can do this all by yourself

See the antiderivative of e to the x
Is e to the x plus C
A U-substitution will help on the test
To avoid the complexity

Just don't forget to substitute back
To what U is equal to
Just talk to me, you know where I'm at
I'll help you know what to do

$$\frac{d}{dx}\left(e^{x}\right) = e^{x}$$

$$\int e^{x}\,dx = e^{x} + c$$

## Integrating the Natural Log

The Natural Log's derivative
Is equal to one over x
So it's time to take some initiative
Because antiderivatives come next

So the antiderivative of one over x
The Natural Log it equals
The constants C, we put down next
It's just another sequel

A U-substitution will help us out
Please don't substitute me
Just work hard, I have no doubt
With practice you'll succeed!


## Trig Integration

Integrating functions, sine or cosine
Is nothing really big
There's no need for Einstein
When integrating Trig

Just for starters, the antiderivative
Of cosine equals sine
Sine's antiderivative is not intuitive
It's the negative of cosine

Substituting U, no, not me
Will help to simplify
An easier problem you will see
There is no need to cry

Don't forget to add the C
It's something we must do
With some practice, you will see
You'll get through this one too

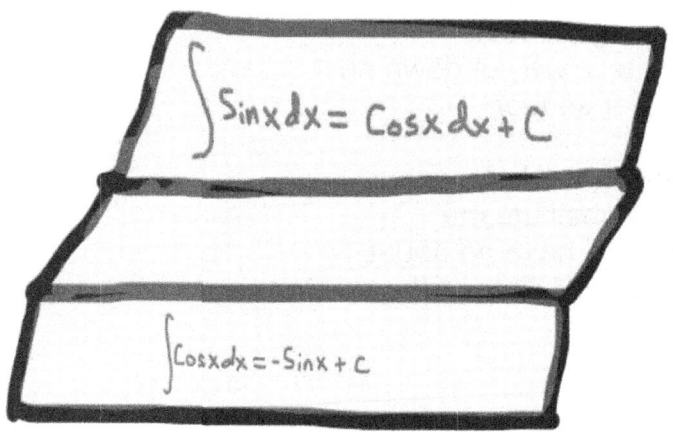

$$\int \sin x \, dx = \cos x \, dx + C$$

$$\int \cos x \, dx = -\sin x + C$$

# Appendix: Study Tips that Work!

## Study Tip 1: Set Academic Goals

It was once written some thousands of years ago, "A man without a goal is a spiritually dead man." I don't know the exact origination of this quote. My grandmother told me this when I was a child. But if we look at what this means in today's context, it may sound something like this: "A person without a goal can't be motivated." Think of an athlete who endures brutal workout and practice routines. As an athlete knows they must endure many hardships to achieve what they want; so-too will a student who has set academic goals do the difficult things required to be successful in the classroom. Students who set academic goals have higher average GPAs than those do not. Set daily, weekly, monthly, quarterly, yearly and long-term academic goals. Then mentally prepare yourself for the hard work and sacrifice that it will take. Your goals can range from simple daily goals, to the more thought-out, long-term goals.

Setting Academic Goals:

- Imagine yourself 5-10 years from now;
    - Where will you be?
    - What type of work will you be doing?
    - Will you find contentment?
    - How does working hard in school help you achieve the things you want in life?
- Set goals for things like attendance and always being prepared for class.
- Always get work done on time.
- Do your best, everyday, inside and outside of the classroom.

# Study Tip 2: Be Aware of Your Own Attitude

Like a rudder that guides the ship along its journey, so do our attitudes guide our lives. Studies show a strong correlation between attitude and success. Think of an athlete preparing for an event or an employee seeking a promotion. Ever hear the phrase, "you need to have a winning attitude"?. There are many that live by the quote "If you have a negative attitude about a future outcome in your life, it will usually come true." For example, you'll never see a successful athlete who doubts their abilities or goes into every game thinking they're going to lose.

Caution: Negative Attitudes are Contagious
Example: While enrolling in next year's math class, you overhear a student who had the same math class and teacher the year before, saying all kinds of negative things. You are immediately overwhelmed with dread, and over the next couple of weeks your negative feelings evolve into sheer anxiety.

Bad attitudes like the example described above are almost never your own; like a bad cold, you catch it from someone else. There are many reasons why a student may not like a particular class. Maybe they were tardy every day, never did homework, or paid attention to the lessons. Try to think of students who took the class and were successful, and always ask yourself the question, "Why can't I be that successful one?

Be aware of your own attitude; and if it is bad, revisit your goals and recommit yourself to them. If you think positively put on a smile, then before you know it, your bad attitude is gone.

Don't be infected by the negative attitudes of others; instead, keep looking towards your goals and try to stay positive.

## Study Tip 3: Be in the Here and Now

Example: Upon arriving to school, Sarah realized she left the milk out on the kitchen counter, and when she gets home from school, she is bound to get a lecture on kitchen responsibility. When she got to math class, it was all she could think about; she texted her friends for moral support, and mentally rehearsed what she was going to say when she got home. She didn't understand or remember much of what went on in class that day, because she was so preoccupied with her dilemma. It is human nature to occasionally get preoccupied with things over which we have no control. Unfortunately for Sarah, she now has even more to be preoccupied with, like all she missed by not being mentally present during the school day. To be in the here and now means to mentally focus on the things in front of you; that is, what you can control. During class, there was nothing Sarah could do about the milk left on the counter; thinking about it just caused her more trouble by falling behind in school. Successful students ignore the negative distractions that occur outside the classroom. They put away computers or phones, unless they are being used for class. Be in the "Here and Now!"

# Study Tip 4: Avoiding Distraction

Studies have shown that students who sit in the front two rows of a college classroom have GPAs that average 15% higher than everyone else.  Most people at first attribute this to the idea that more motivated students sit up front. But this wasn't  the case; the reason was that people who sat farther back were subconsciously distracted by the backs of other people's heads. Everything a person sees competes with the learning process, and this is enough to make a difference in overall average GPA. What is interesting is that sometimes, something we're not even aware of can have a measurable difference on how well we are able to learn.

Even little distractions make a big difference:

- What kind of distractive affect would it be to text friends during a lesson?
- A conversation during a math lesson?

Focus on the here and now:

- Do everything you can to focus and avoid distractions.
- Get involved with everything going on in class, i.e. participate in discussions, listen to other peoples questions, and try to think of your own.
- Make being focused during class a daily goal.
- Pay attention and stay focused, even if you totally get the topic or understand the problem.

## Study Tip 5: Before or After?

Did you know that reviewing notes and homework 3-5 minutes before a math or science class increases comprehension of the new lesson by as much as 60 percent? To get the same benefit in an English or humanities type of class, do your review within 3-5 minutes after class.

Who would've known?

Now, of course, this doesn't mean it is okay to be tardy to English class. The first five minutes of any teacher's instruction is usually the most crucial Don't forget the little things that you do will add up, and make a big difference.

## Study Tip 6: Try to Work Ahead

Your brain is like a filing cabinet, storing away memories and experiences into different compartments according to its type for easier recall. There is actually a memory technique where if you forget something, you think of everything related to whatever it was you forgot. By doing this, you activate the part of the brain where the memory is stored, possibly triggering recall.

As a student, your brain has to work overtime. Every day it is exposed to different lessons, points of views, homework, social life, discussions, etc. It has to evaluate every bit of new information, determine whether it is important enough to be stored, and then where to store it. Try to imagine a dumpster full of papers thrown in the middle of floor. It's a huge pile of papers, but only a portion is worth keeping; the rest need to be recycled. The important pieces of paper need to be filed away in case they are needed later. This is why it takes the brain 24-72 hours to make sense of new information. Sometimes when teaching a concept that was taught in a previous course, I get comments like, "Why didn't they explain it this way before?" And I'll always tell them, your brain has just had more time to understand. So, how does this knowledge of how the brain stores and metabolizes new information help the student get better grades?

Think of two students, Kong and Sarah:
Using the course syllabus, Kong determines what the lesson will be two days from now. He then reads the lesson and examples from the text, goes online, finds example video lessons on the topic, and then attempts some of the homework. By the day of the lesson, Kong already knows exactly what his questions are going to be. He then follows the lesson intently, even during parts he understood before, always looking for an opportunity to get involved and participate.

Now Sarah, she's about a half a lesson or so behind, it's been a couple of days and now the previous lesson is just beginning to make sense to her. But this new lesson has her head in a "whirlwind," and she can't even formulate a question.

In the above example, there are no differences between Kong's and Sarah's abilities. But the small difference between being slightly behind in a math class vs. being slightly ahead is going to make a major difference in the learning outcome.

Kong's brain had the advantage in that his brain had been thinking about it long before Sarah's. It's like running a race, giving the other person a 20-minute head start and expecting to win. Personally, out of any study habit I have known, nothing is more effective than working ahead, if you can.

## Study Tip 7: Test Preparation

*Doing homework, attending class, and, oh, the test! Everything comes down to this one moment, a single frame in the movie of our academic lives. Class discussions, participation, homework and projects,yet the test outweighs them all. Teachers remind us every day; the most important event on the calendar they say.*

It seems unfair that all the hard work in a particular class can be evaluated by just a few simple tests and quizzes, especially if you are like many students who claim they are just no good at taking tests. But we also need to face the fact that testing is not going away soon. Yes, alternative means of assessing students have been explored for decades now, and with all that, we just can't get away from testing. Nobody is going to get through college without having to take a test at some point.

So what about the students who are poor at testing? If a student has been identified as having a test anxiety issue, and there is an accommodation plan in place, then the teacher follows the plan. But studies have shown that the overwhelming majority of bad test-takers have anxiety only because they are not prepared to take the test. Yes, lack of preparation is the major cause of test anxiety. Test preparation is something all students should learn to do. There are online books on how to get good grades, and they usually have a section about test preparation.

**Test Preparation Tips**

- Prepare as if the test or quiz was a day before the scheduled date. If the test is next Thursday, pretend it is really scheduled for Wednesday.
- Test preparation is not simply done the night before; it is an ongoing process that is done daily.
- Listen to your teacher for hints and clues as to what may be on the test, and take notes.

- Create a comprehensive list of anything that could be testable. For example, finding the roots using the quadratic formula is something testable.
- Keep up on your daily and weekly reviews. Then re-review everything from the comprehensive test list.
- Make sure you know how to do everything on the list of what may be tested.
- Review any extra notes, homework or any miscellaneous items.
- Have good diet, exercise and sleep habits.

## During Test

- Show up early for class on the day of the test.
- Have all tools, calculators, paper, and extra pencils ready to go before class starts.
- Read all instruction and questions carefully.
- Do all of the easier problems first, skipping anything that you think may cause some trouble. After the easier ones are done, then go back to the more difficult problems.
- Always review your work before handing it in.

# Study Tip 8: Daily Review

Studies show that within 24 hours, students forget 75 to 80 percent of everything learned in class on a particular day. However, if the student does a 10 to 15 minute daily review, retention goes up to over 80 percent. A daily review could include immediately attempting math homework after class or when you get home, or glancing over examples, old homework or notes. For some subjects, it's a great idea to find other classmates to have a quick 10 to 20 minute reflection about class.

One thing to be cautious about, especially for the weekend, is getting certain homework like math done too quickly, then doing nothing for several days after. For example, during Friday's math class you found the lesson easy, and completed all work within 15 minutes, then did nothing until the following Monday. If you do this, by Monday you will have lost most of your gains in the subject.

It's not enough to say "I have no homework for a particular class, so I can take the day off in that particular subject"; a daily review for all classes should be a daily ritual. **Students who get good grades study even when they don't have homework.**

# Study Tip 9: Weekly Reviews

If you want to bring your retention to at least 90 percent, you must do a weekly review for every class. In just 10 to 15 minutes you can review all the notes, homework, papers, reports, books, chapters read and more. The positive effects of daily and weekly reviews cannot be overstated. For the small amount of extra time it takes one day per week, the payout in retention and understanding is huge. The benefits of the weekly review are so great that the time spent in doing it is often offset by how much less time you'll need in a week because you are prepared. It's interesting, because those who plan their study time on an as-needed basis usually end up putting in more overall study time, and with less benefit, than those who conduct daily, weekly, and monthly reviews on a continual basis. Just remember to follow your periodic review schedule, and you will be surprised by the progress you make towards your goals.

Extra tip: Most courses have a cutoff of at least 90 % in order to earn an A, but conducting a weekly review only brings retention to an average of 90 %. So, what if you are trying to earn an A, and you don't want to cut it so close? What some people do is review beyond what is required for the class. This could be pursuing a topic deeper, or doing extra homework from the text, going on the internet, or even learning more of what is required. For example: If you just go an extra 10% beyond what is required, your average retention is now 90% of 110%, which is like an overall 99%. Get the idea?

## Study Tip 10: Quarterly Reviews

By now everyone has heard that cramming for final exams is not a good study practice. But this is true only for those who rely on the cram as their sole means for review. To the student who has mastered the daily, weekly, and monthly review system, preparing for a final is just another review day of, perhaps, 15-20 minutes. It is recommended that several sessions take place only when studying for a major assessment.

Example: When studying for a math test, look at old homework and quizzes, read through examples and rework some of the earlier homework. Key in on any topics your instructor may have emphasized during previous instruction. Also, don't forget to prepare as if the test is one day prior to when it actually happens. Revisit Study Tip 7 for a more comprehensive list.

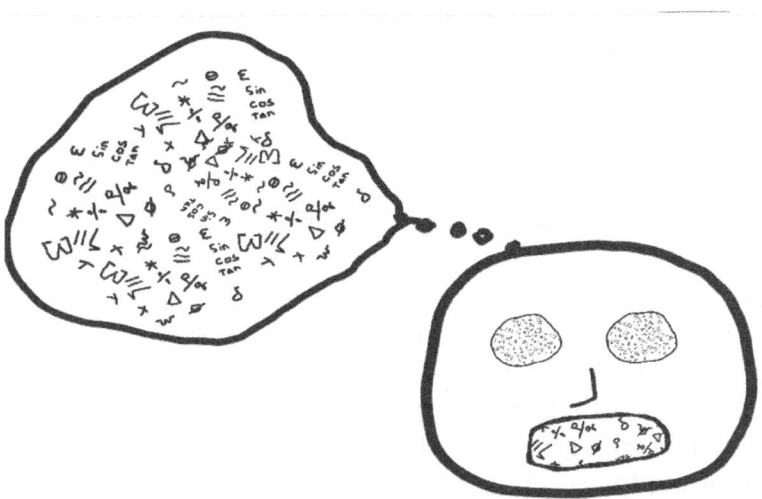

**Quarterly reviews help you keep it all together. .**

## Study Tip 11: Scheduling Breaks

You're studying for an important test or you have an extra-long reading assignment that you just want to get through. It is tempting at this point to want to plunge through without a break to save time. But are you really saving time? Studies show that the brain can only stay focused for up to 50-minute intervals, followed by mindless 10-minute breaks. Therefore, anything beyond 50 minutes without a break is wasted effort. Two 50-minute study sessions with appropriate breaks are actually more effective than 6 to 8 hours straight with few to no breaks at all.

## Study Tip 12: Never Tune Out

Bobby realizes that Mr. H's lesson was about a topic he learned last year, so he tunes out and uses the opportunity to get caught up on other stuff and takes a mental vacation by playing games on his phone. Much to Bobby's disappointment, he fails the next test. He swears up and down that he knew the stuff, and was surprised at how little he remembered.

Situations like Bobby's are common. When in college, taking calculus for the first time really worried me. Many students in the class had already taken calculus in high school. I assumed I would be at a disadvantage, but what surprised me was that it appeared that those who took the course in high school did not perform as well as those who hadn't.

One possible reason for this is that while our brains are primed to recall big picture ideas, overall topics, and lessons learned, it finds details less important. It's like remembering that you had lunch two days ago, but not remembering what you ate. The only problem is the test will be on what we had for lunch.

When taking a class, remember to always pay attention as if it were the first time you have ever heard the topic or question. Otherwise, you too will forget the details of what is needed on the test. Remember, the more you are exposed to a topic, the closer it gets to long-term memory. So don't forget to pay attention, even if you think you don't need to.

## Study Tip 13: No Such Thing as Luck

Never rely on dishonest measures such as cheating. Studies show that people who rely on cheating are statistically almost 2 GPA points lower than those who rely on their own honest efforts, and even worse, they drop out of college at almost 5 times the rate. Think of taking a state math exam where 60 percent of the participants get a particular question wrong; what are your chances of copying the correct answer from the person next to you? What will happen when you get to the next level class and you really don't know the stuff because of cheating? Your best chances are always better through honest hard work and effort.  Just follow the other study tips throughout this book, and you will have no trouble preparing honestly, with no luck.

## Study Tip 14: Don't Wait!

Michael didn't understand Monday's lesson on multiplying binomials. He said, "I'll come after school Friday and get some extra help." On Tuesday the factoring lesson was taught. Since factoring is the inverse of multiplying, he probably had trouble understanding factoring. He also likely had trouble with Wednesday's solve quadratics by factoring lesson, and by the time Thursday's lesson comes along, Michael may be totally lost in the class.

Now, because one lesson is connected to the one before, Michael will probably need help for everything covered during the week. Even worse, depending on the level of the high school or college course, Michael could get to a point where he is hopelessly behind, a true but unfortunate fact, and it could happen to any of us if we let down our guard.

Now, if the problem was fixed Monday, at the onset of the trouble, Michael may have never fallen behind to begin with. By getting Monday's lesson down while it is still Monday means that he'll have an easier time with Tuesday's lesson. On any of the given days of the week Michael needs help, he should try to get the help on that day. It's not always possible, but every effort should be made. If you can't make it after school, try to connect with a friend, or just go online and search for what it is you need help with. With the resources available at our fingertips, there is rarely a reason to fall behind.

# Study Tip 15: Manage Your Time Wisely

During math class, Joeann realizes the teacher is covering a lesson she heard before. What a great time, she thinks, to get some reading done on Civil War history. Or maybe, she can take a mental break, catch up on a text, or play a game. After all, the teacher is talking about a subject she already knows. Two weeks later Joeann is scratching her head, wondering what went wrong on the math test. She thought she knew everything that was taught over the last couple weeks. In fact, it was one of the easier units of the year.

Tuning out in the middle of a class, because it's a subject you already know, violates many of the study tips throughout this book. Like avoiding distraction, and staying focused. Does an athlete who spends hours focusing before an event turn it off and on like a light switch? No. The same is true when we try to go in and out of focus during a class discussion or lesson, it just does not work.

## TIP

Make a schedule, and set out blocks of time to achieve certain objectives, such as a reading or writing assignment. Studies show that most of us will take the time given to us to accomplish any task. For example, if we are given 4 weeks to complete a project that really takes 3 days, we'll usually take 4 weeks or more to do it. Instead, if we set out blocks of time, and make it a goal to get it done during that time, we will be much more likely to finish the project in the 3 days needed.

# Study Tip 16: Listen to People's Questions

Jerome asked a question about a math problem that Jill already had worked out. So while the instructor went over the problem with the class, Jill thought it would be a good time to catch up with a text from a friend. Unfortunately, Jill got an almost identical question wrong on the test two weeks later. What happened?

Students sometimes think that if it wasn't a question they thought of, or pertaining to a problem they had trouble with, they are excused from interacting with the question and response. The problem, especially in math, is there could be ways of thinking that you may not have thought of before, maybe another method. Plus, if you want to get the concept into your long-term memory, you need as many interactions with the concept as you can get. All questions from all students should be treated as an opportunity to engage with the topic and deepen your understanding.

Always Stay Tuned In

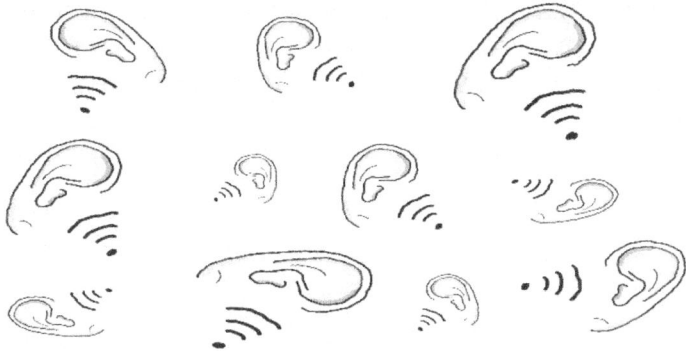

## Study Tip 17: Think of Questions to Ask

Asking questions in front of our peers or in a large classroom can make anyone feel uncomfortable. There is always the risk (we may believe) that someone may think our question was dumb, or we just may feel uncomfortable speaking out in large group settings. Unfortunately, having unanswered questions will make it very difficult to understand what is going on. So, the bottom line is we need to ask questions or find some alternative means for getting them answered. When I was in college, I remember how uncomfortable I was at first, but after a while, I got used to asking questions. Others may later thank you for asking the question, because it was one they had. Studies show, that no matter what the question, 20-40% actually had the same question themselves, but either didn't think of the question at first, or we're shy to ask.
For math class developing and getting answers to questions is an important part of the learning process. Always attempt every problem in your homework and get help with any problem that gives you trouble. And remember the importance of listening to other people's questions.

## Study Tip 18: Have Good Attendance

Missing as little as one day a week can lower a student's GPA. There is a strong correlation between attendance and grades. Also, remember Study Tip 5? How are you going to study your math notes 3-5 minutes before class if you are absent or tardy?

For the last couple of years, I have been posting all my lessons online, so if a student is absent, they can watch the lesson from home. I do have a few absent students who watch the online lessons, and do well on the homework and tests. But the majority of those who are absent do not do very well. Maybe it's because they're not concerned enough to watch the online lessons. Or, maybe there is another reason for not attending class. The practice of posting lessons online was always intended as a supplement, not a replacement to attending class. Remember, the more interactions, the deeper the understanding and long-term memory on the subject. Attending class is extremely important; in fact, those who interact with the subject material in the classroom are more likely to remember long-term than those who just watch the lesson online.

Also, being tardy to a class is like getting off on the wrong foot in a journey. Try to be in every class a couple of minutes early with the focus on preparing for the lesson. Get off on the right foot, and complete your journey.

## Study Tip 19: Make Use of Every Minute

Tic toc, tic toc … seconds add to minutes, minutes to hours, and hours to days. Just 5 minutes wasted per day adds up to over an hour in just two weeks, or over 30 hours in a year. Some people waste hours per day. Do they have any idea what those wasted hours add up to? How much more could they have gotten done if they applied those hours to something productive?

Try to think of moments throughout the day where you are not doing anything, like waiting for a bus, riding the light rail, or maybe waiting in a long line somewhere. We call this opportunity time. These are perfect opportunities to pull out your notes, and conduct daily, weekly or even monthly reviews.

Just 30 minutes per day of opportunity time, gives you 7 hours of extra review time every two weeks!

## Study Tip 20: Teach another Person

Teachers from all subject areas understand that the teacher always learns more than the student. Anytime you have to break down a concept for another to understand, your own understanding deepens in a very permanent way. So find a friend or younger sibling, and teach them your new concepts. Join a study group, and take every opportunity to interact and explain your own reasoning. When in class, participate to the fullest. When I was in college, while participating in class, I would always look for someone who needed help with a problem. When attempting to help, my own understanding increased. In some cases, I didn't even know how to do the problem before volunteering to explain. The funny thing was that in the process of explaining, I would simultaneously reason it out. By breaking it down for another person, I was actually breaking it down for myself. Give this a try sometime, and you will surprise yourself.

# Study Tip 21: Do Every Problem

Jeremy thinks he's good at doing homework, and on any given assignment, he does most of it. On his last assignment, for example, he did 27 out of 30 problems. There were many opportunities to get help on the three missed problems, but 27 out of 30 seemed good enough. In Jeremy's mind, missing a problem here or there, or not completely understanding all the concepts was good enough, as long as he got most of it. Unfortunately, Jeremy failed the upcoming unit test, and he had no idea why. He did most of the homework, but on the test, it was as if he didn't know anything. So what is going on here? This is a perfect example of how small things done on a regular basis can have a significant overall impact. 27 out of 30, or 90 percent, would be a great score on most tests. But most high school math teachers assign homework daily; therefore, 27 out of 30 is the same as missing 3 problems a day; and after 10 days, that's 30 missed problems. It's like going into a test with 30 unanswered questions. Not a recipe for success. Therefore, DO ALL ASSIGNED WORK – 100% of it. Get immediate help with any homework you do not understand.

## Study Tip 22: Never Fall Behind

It would be hard to believe you were following the other study tips, especially the important one about working ahead, if you fell behind. In some college courses, getting caught up is almost impossible, because a great deal of work is piled on daily. Therefore, do everything in your power to never fall behind. If you don't overload your schedule, you should be able to manage it, stay caught up and, hopefully, a little ahead.

If, in circumstances beyond your control, you fall behind, talk to each of your teachers about your circumstances, and see if they will assist you in a catch-up plan.

The plan should include doing the most current assignment first, followed by one of the late assignments. The number of late assignments would then equal the approximate number of days it would take to get caught up in the class.

Mr. H after raking some leaves.

## Study Tip 23: Build Yourself Up

When any person makes up a schedule, the first thing they must consider is; do they have time for everything they put on it? Do not expect that just because you signed up for seven AP classes, joined two clubs, work a job, babysit at home, and play a sport, that everyone should slow down in order for you to keep up. When we pick a schedule, we become responsible for what we put on it and can no longer complain about how busy we are. A mistake people make when first entering college is setting a course schedule with too many advanced level classes. The workload becomes too heavy for them to manage, sometimes causing them to drop the program altogether.
If we instead, choose something that is manageable, like some elective courses for the new college student, or an easier schedule for the highschooler, we will then build ourselves up, and over time, we will be able to manage heavier and heavier course loads.

## Study Tip 24: Use the Internet

For mathematics, you can find a video presentation for almost any lesson ever taught. The internet is a tremendous resource for students of today's era. Just remember that the internet should always be used to supplement, not replace, what happens in class. Nothing replaces good classroom participation, because the more you interact with new knowledge, the more you own it. Remember, all of the positive things you do on behalf of your learning add together and will have a big overall impact.

## Study Tip 25: Graphing Calculators

Calculators are to mathematicians as tools are to mechanics. The various features included with most modern calculators allow mathematicians to solve problems that would normally be unsolvable by hand; and without the right tools, a mechanic would encounter many problems that would be unfixable.

Students in high school or college are likely to encounter an occasional math test, and having the proper materials, such as a calculator, sharpened pencil etc., can be an important part of being prepared. Now, imagine a mechanic off to a job, and he has only sixty minutes get the job done. He forgot his tool box at home, so he grabs a random one from the shed. When he gets to the job, he has trouble because he is not familiar with the tool box – he spends a lot of time looking through it to find the right tools. Now, imagine borrowing someone else's calculator on the way to the ACT exam. Get the idea? There is nothing better than having your own calculator that you have already practiced on.

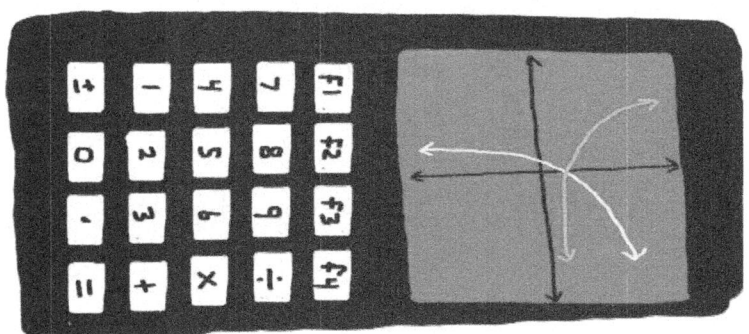

## Study Tip 26: Learn to Power Read

Reading a textbook for a high school or college course is not the same as reading a newspaper, or a fiction novel at a coffee shop. If not done properly, hours of time can be wasted. For reading textbooks, you want to learn to power read. Power reading is when you, to your fullest ability, engage the text with all of your body, mind and spirit. Here is a checklist that may help you get started.

- Find a chair that sits upright in an area of low distraction, and a table at comfortable height.
- Read the title of the chapter about to be read, then try to guess, as much as possible, what it is about.
- If there are summary questions at the end of the reading, ponder these before reading.
- Read the chapter summary.
- Read all the subheadings within the chapter, and try to guess what they are about.

Once the checklist is complete, read the chapter while monitoring your comprehension. Monitoring your comprehension is when you pay attention to how well you are understanding and following the text. Since our brain learns to decode words automatically, a person can go on reading for quite a period, while thinking of other things.

For example, while reading a textbook you notice that you day-dreamed through the last couple pages. The remedy now is to trace back to where you last comprehended. Then, go slightly back from that point, and then continue to read from that point onward. Repeat this process every time you lose focus on what you are reading. Sort of like two steps forward and one step back.

Highlighting is no longer recommended; what is suggested now is to summarize main points onto post-it notes as you read, and then stick them to the pages where they are on. It may be more work at first, but think of how efficient your weekly review would be when all you have to do is flip the pages reading post-it notes.

Sometimes when reading math-related material, it is normal to read the same page five or more times. You would never see a person at a coffee table reading a magazine like this. Power reading is for academic purposes only.

# Study Tip 27: Learn to Power Focus

Related to power reading but in the context of a classroom lesson, to power focus simply means to monitor how well you are paying attention to the lesson without drifting off mentally. To power focus, think mentally in anticipation, like you are getting ready to run a race, and you are anticipating the start whistle going off. When power focusing, we are in this heightened state of mind during the entire lesson. It takes effort and energy to work your ability to the level of being able to do this throughout the day. But over time, it will get easier.

## Study Tip 28:Testing Tip: Double-check work

We all make mistakes. On a test, the mistake can simply be a careless one, or maybe we just don't know how to do the problem. Now if you are following all the study tips to this point, it shouldn't be because you don't know how to do the problem. The most common mistakes are the careless ones. For someone who puts all the preparation time into a test, making a careless mistake can be most frustrating. To have a beautiful test brought down to mediocre because of arithmetic or other simple mistakes, is sad. If given time, simply double-checking all answers will eliminate this problem.

Thank you for reading my book
I hope you took more than a look
You see Math is the key
To prosperity
And sometimes it helps when we cook!

Taerg si Htam!! to all!

Michael J Humphrey

Made in the USA
Middletown, DE
23 November 2022

15539147R00066